Praise for *Bridging Differences for Better Mentoring*

"While our similarities give us comfort, it is our differences that give us growth. In many ways, embracing differences is the very essence of learning. *Bridging Differences for Better Mentoring* provides solid guidance through profound wisdom, practical tools, and case examples on how to leverage differences for rich, mutual growth. Mentors and mentees alike will find this book a potent and enjoyable gift."
—**Chip R. Bell, coauthor of *Managers as Mentors***

"There are rare times when a book is written that expands your mind, opens your heart, and touches your soul. This is one of those books. Fain and Zachary, who have a deep knowledge and understanding of the context and processes of mentoring, confront us with our need to view the world and those within it with a broader focus on the breadth and beauty of varied perspectives, which in turn will bring richness to our own perceptions and abilities. If we are to mentor and be mentored in ways that can foster growth and understanding in all involved and in our world, we will take their knowledge and make it our own."
—**Frances Kochan, Wayne T. Smith Distinguished Professor Emerita, Auburn University**

"Alas, all too often mentoring relationships occur through happenstance, and sometimes they work and sometimes they don't. This excellent book cuts through the 'luck' part and guides mentor and mentee into excellent conversations that build their connection and their impact. Yes, there are many mentoring books available, and if you think you've seen it all, give this one a try. Lois and Lisa meld their experiences, know-how, and backgrounds to provide a vast amount of ideas and concepts that are research based and practice tested."
—**Beverly Kaye, bestselling coauthor of *Love 'Em or Lose 'Em***

"Research has shown that mentoring is a wonderful tool, especially for groups that have historically been underrepresented in the workplace. *Bridging Differences for Better Mentoring* is a much-needed resource to build career-enhancing strategies."
—**Mary-Frances Winters, President and CEO, The Winters Group, Inc.**

"*Bridging Differences for Better Mentoring* is a highly accessible and well-written guide for all those interested in upping their mentoring game across cultures and differences. I was particularly impressed by how practical the book is and how carefully the authors ground their insights in social science research. Very useful book!"
—**Andy Molinsky, PhD, Professor of International Management and Organizational Behavior, Brandeis University, and author of *Global Dexterity* and *Reach***

"Building on years of working with individuals and organizations to improve their experiences with mentoring, Lois Zachary and Lisa Fain have created an invaluable resource for those who want to enhance their experiences of mentoring in an increasingly diverse workforce. They have provided a compelling and simple structure for building self-awareness, becoming an outstanding mentoring partner through demonstrating genuine curiosity, asking good questions, and establishing routines in a mentoring partnership that lead to deep trust, growth-enhancing conversations, and transformational outcomes. At the core, the structure and methods presented in this book enable the reader to become culturally competent and to lean in to differences and leverage them, rather than deny or minimize their potential value."
—**Kathy E. Kram, PhD, Shipley Professor in Management Emerita, Questrom School of Business, Boston University**

"Bridging Differences for Better Mentoring is a nuanced and instructive reflection of the modern workplace and a necessary resource for today's leaders. Equipped with invaluable experience and universal strategies, Fain and Zachary offer insight into connecting across differences and leveraging everyone's unique strengths—a critical skill set that every inclusive leader should develop. Complete with real stories and actionable steps, this book will resonate with both mentors and mentees alike."

—Jennifer Brown, founder, CEO, and President, Jennifer Brown Consulting

"Bridging Differences for Better Mentoring is a road map for building successful mentoring relationships. Every chapter illustrates examples of how key concepts play out in real life and introduces the reader to reflective exercises to assist in integrating the wisdom into practice. This insightful book also adeptly addresses issues of bias and power positions to help establish inclusive and more comfortable relationships. Combining experiences and generational perspectives, Lisa and Lois have written the ultimate go-to guide on how to bridge differences in a mentoring relationship."

—Marcia Reynolds, PsyD, global expert in executive coaching and author of *The Discomfort Zone*

"A rare and much-needed contribution, this timely book brings leaders and educators down-to-earth advice on a pressing and little-understood aspect of mentorship. Using fresh and accessible language and blending practical ideas with current research, the authors demonstrate their deep experience on every page. Essential reading for mentors—aspiring and experienced alike."

—Laurent A. Daloz, author of *Mentor* and coauthor of *Common Fire*

"Lisa Fain and Lois Zachary have used their world-class expertise to provide a road map for leaders to more effectively connect, learn, and grow through mentoring. Highly recommended!"

—Doug Bruhnke, founder and CEO, Global Chamber

"Regardless of where you are in your career's trajectory, this unique guide offers the wisdom and real-life applications for the furtherance of empathic leadership skills of both mentors and mentees."

—John Hensing, MD, FACP, retired Chief Clinical Officer, Banner Health

"Fain and Zachary's book expands, integrates, and elevates their previous work in mentoring and cultural competence, using case studies and interactive exercises to engage and challenge readers to explore ways to create more inclusive mentoring relationships in their own contexts. I look forward to applying the valuable insights I have gained through this book to our Young Innovators Project, in which we are training K–12 educators nationwide to more effectively mentor the diverse and creative students in their schools."

—Ruth V. Small, PhD, Laura J. and L. Douglas Meredith Professor Emerita, School of Information Studies, Syracuse University, and Director, The Young Innovators Project

BRIDGING DIFFERENCES *for* BETTER MENTORING

*Lean Forward,
Learn,
and Leverage*

Lisa Z. Fain
and
Lois J. Zachary

BK
Berrett–Koehler Publishers, Inc.

BRIDGING DIFFERENCES
for BETTER MENTORING

*Lean Forward,
Learn,
and Leverage*

Lisa Z. Fain

and

Lois J. Zachary

BK

Berrett–Koehler Publishers, Inc.

Berrett-Koehler Publishers, Inc.
1333 Broadway, Suite 1000
Oakland, CA 94612-1921
Tel: (510) 817-2277 / Fax: (510) 817-2278
www.bkconnection.com

ORDERING INFORMATION

QUANTITY SALES.
Special discounts are available on quantity purchases by corporations, associations, and others. For details, contact the "Special Sales Department" at the Berrett-Koehler address above.

INDIVIDUAL SALES.
Berrett-Koehler publications are available through most bookstores. They can also be ordered directly from Berrett-Koehler: Tel: (800) 929-2929; Fax: (802) 864-7626; www.bkconnection.com.

ORDERS FOR COLLEGE TEXTBOOK/COURSE ADOPTION USE.
Please contact Berrett-Koehler: Tel: (800) 929-2929; Fax: (802) 864-7626.

Distributed to the US trade and internationally by Penguin Random House Publisher Services.

Berrett-Koehler and the BK logo are registered trademarks of Berrett-Koehler Publishers, Inc.

Printed in the United States

Berrett-Koehler books are printed on long-lasting acid-free paper. When it is available, we choose paper that has been manufactured by environmentally responsible processes. These may include using trees grown in sustainable forests, incorporating recycled paper, minimizing chlorine in bleaching, or recycling the energy produced at the paper mill.

Library of Congress Cataloging-in-Publication Data

Names: Fain, Lisa Z., author. | Zachary, Lois J., author.
Title: Bridging differences for better mentoring : lean forward, learn, and leverage /
Lisa Z. Fain and Lois J. Zachary.
Description: First edition. | Oakland, CA : Berrett-Koehler Publishers,
[2020] | Includes bibliographical references and index.
Identifiers: LCCN 2019038545 | ISBN 9781523085897 (paperback) |
ISBN 9781523085903 (pdf) | ISBN 9781523085910 (epub)
Subjects: LCSH: Mentoring in business. | Diversity in the workplace. | Intercultural communication.
Classification: LCC HF5385 .F35 2020 | DDC 658.3/124—dc23
LC record available at https://lccn.loc.gov/2019038545

FIRST EDITION

28 27 26 25 24 23 22 21 20 || 10 9 8 7 6 5 4 3 2 1

Book producer: BookMatters
Text designer: BookMatters
Cover designer: Nicole Hayward
Copyeditor: Amy Smith Bell
Proofer: Janet Reed Blake
Indexer: Leonard Rosenbaum

To David and Ed,
our wonderfully supportive spouses, wingmen, cheerleaders,
and supporters.

To Talia and Emily,
our respective children and grandchildren, for your patience
with the sacrifices of time and energy this process has
demanded. You inspired us to write a book to create a better
workplace for you.

To Lois (from Lisa),
whose leadership in the field of mentoring I have only
come to appreciate as an adult, but from which I benefited
throughout my life. What a joy, an honor, and a privilege to
have created something with you and to share this passion.

To Lisa (from Lois),
whose creativity, grit, and smarts added so much to our
collaborative endeavor. I've learned so much from you.
Thank you for all you've done and will continue to do to
make this a better world.

CONTENTS

FIGURES AND TABLES

Figures

Tables

FOREWORD

We have known about the importance of mentoring for developing people and organizations for several decades. Organizations are more frequently turning to mentoring as a solution for a range of their needs, from early socialization to talent management to leadership development. Despite acknowledging the power of mentoring, few organizations have successfully leveraged it as part of their overall strategy. Many individuals report not having access to the benefits of mentoring, and this lack of access is especially true for women and people of color. There is also an ongoing debate over the value of "formal" mentoring, with many arguing that it is less effective than informal, self-determined types of mentoring. Thus, despite its popularity, organization-sponsored mentoring often lacks inclusion, leaving out those individuals who should benefit the most from these powerful developmental relationships.

My own research and work with organizations over the past three decades has focused on the importance of mentoring as not only a tool for developing people and organizations but also a transformational process for creating understanding, strengthening relationships, and sharing knowledge among diverse groups of people and cultures. This work has convinced me that there is no more powerful tool than mentoring to unleash the power of diversity and inclusion in ways that benefit people and organizations. Thus it was a pleasure and honor to read this unique work and offer my insights and perspective.

Bridging Differences for Better Mentoring is a timely, evidence-based, and practical discussion of the power of mentoring to support, leverage, and advance diversity and inclusion across all different types of organizations. Lisa Fain and Lois Zachary leverage their combined research and practical knowledge with hundreds of mentors and mentees to provide insight into how we can better utilize mentoring as a transformational tool for individuals and organizational leaders. *Bridging*

Differences is not merely a book title, but a call to action for scholars, leaders, and management practitioners to unleash the power of mentoring for creating a more inclusive organizational culture and social system. The work that provides the foundation of this book reminds us to move beyond the ease of one-shot mentoring efforts that are based on the myth of a single mentor or sponsor and toward developing effective and sustainable efforts as the key to success that are grounded in both research and best practice.

Bridging Differences is a strategy that can be used to support individual development as well as organizational transformation. To accomplish this, the authors examine the ways in which individuals should prepare for the work of mentoring. The book is organized into three parts: lean forward into differences, learn from differences, and leverage differences. Each section includes knowledge that the authors have gained from organizational practice, individual coaching, and research on mentoring. Each section of the book gave me valuable insight into three keys to unlocking the power of mentoring as a tool for diversity and inclusion: purpose, process, and participation.

In Part 1, "Lean Forward into Differences," the authors signal that we need to prepare ourselves for the work of mentoring. They remind us that we must first focus on the purpose for mentoring: to cultivate meaningful relationships. Although this may seem obvious and perhaps easy, it becomes more complicated as individuals attempt to build relationships across differences. Through their mentoring framework, the authors challenge us to not simply "accept" differences but to actually see them, acknowledge them, and understand how these differences impact our mentoring relationships. This means building our knowledge around culture and identity, especially for those whose experiences are vastly different from our own. It also means developing the capacity to face barriers that interfere with the purpose of mentoring, such as all forms of bias and privilege.

The model presented by the authors prompts us to understand the link between mentoring purpose and the specific mentoring tool or program that can best fit the needs of the organization, team, or workplace culture. Too often, we think of mentoring in a homogeneous fashion that takes the power out of the diversity of mentoring structures, types, functions, and methods we have at our disposal. *Bridging Differences* means spending a significant amount of time preparing ourselves for mentoring, which begins with clarity and consensus on its purpose.

"Learn from Differences" is covered in Part 2, where the authors guide us through the ways in which mentoring unlocks knowledge about commonalities, diversity, worldviews, and innovative perspectives. Then we explore how we share and transfer this invaluable knowledge. This means paying attention to the process of mentoring both from an individual and especially from an organizational perspective. The process of communication, exchange, and knowledge transfer can either be facilitated or blocked by how we engage in the process of learning across differences. Here the authors spend necessary time with practice tools in a deep dive into the impact of effective communication across differences. In my work with organizations it has become clear that communication as process also must fit with the organization's culture. Understanding how decisions are made, how successful initiatives have been done in the past, and gaining clarity on the "unspoken rules" within the organization is always part of the work that must be done for effective mentoring across differences to take place. The authors remind us that there is no universal solution to learning across differences. We can't merely do "some mentoring," copy what has worked for other companies, or purchase a predesigned product. Learning from differences means committing to developing understanding within the mentoring relationships, which also means developing our ability to deal with the inevitable conflict resolving from diverse relationships. Each chapter within Part 2 provides valuable and practical tools for how to learn from differences as a commitment to the mentoring process.

In Part 3, "Leverage Differences," the authors explore what it takes to get full utilization and impact from diverse mentoring relationships. This section offers practical guidance and tools that can be customized for our own unique mentoring relationships. The authors examine such key issues as understanding and agreements among the mentor-mentee, goal setting, and outcomes. These practical tools remind us that effective mentoring across differences requires that we put forth effort to ensure that there is mutual participation. Perhaps this is where some formal programs lose their impact. We match individuals together, have a flashy program rollout, then leave mentors and mentees on their own to navigate these complex relationships without guidance, tools, or ongoing support.

The chapters in this part of the book provide tested tools that can be accessed across many different relationships that one will have over time to help them navigate, learn, and leverage mentoring. I found the space for reflection, case studies of mentoring pairs, and "Your Turn" exercises to be essential tools in helping to develop and maintain meaningful mentoring relationships across differences that can be used repeatedly across time and experience. These practical tools remind us that participation is the essential building block of meaningful diverse mentoring relationships and requires our knowledgeable engagement.

I learned many valuable lessons from reading this work by Fain and Zachary. The authors reminded me that mentoring is most effective when individuals (and organizations) make a total commitment that moves beyond merely discussing diversity and toward bridging differences. This means taking advantage of the practical knowledge and tools they have provided to develop a personal portfolio of tools and strategies that can build and sustain meaningful mentoring relationships, promote collaboration across differences, and link mentoring to such core values as diversity and inclusion. The valuable lesson I learned is that mentoring is most effective when there is also a total commitment to both mentoring and diversity. There is no quick fix, single design, or magic technology for mentoring to be effective. However, Fain and Zachary have provided an evidence-based set of tools, techniques, and approaches to assist with the vital work of mentoring as we build bridges across our differences.

Audrey J. Murrell, PhD
ACTING DEAN, UNIVERSITY HONORS COLLEGE
PROFESSOR OF BUSINESS ADMINISTRATION, PSYCHOLOGY, PUBLIC AND
INTERNATIONAL AFFAIRS
UNIVERSITY OF PITTSBURGH

PREFACE

Welcome! You are about to begin an exciting and eye-opening process during which you will explore your own cultural lens, recognize the myriad of differences you and your mentoring partner bring to the table, and build skills you can use to bridge differences in your mentoring relationships.

Bridging Differences builds on coauthor Lois Zachary's mentoring philosophy and four-phase mentoring model, and draws from many of her other mentoring publications.[1] Although she has devoted sections of each of her books to understanding difference (especially in *The Mentor's Guide*), none have explored the topic of cultural competency in mentoring in depth. Coauthor Lisa Fain brings her expertise in coaching and cultural competency, and her passion for creating inclusive work environments to her role as CEO of the Center for Mentoring Excellence. Her work focuses on assisting companies to create more inclusive workplaces through mentoring by helping leaders to become more aware of their own cultural framework, to show up authentically, and to lead diverse teams that achieve better results.

Bridging Differences for Better Mentoring represents a marriage of the authors' shared passions for mentoring and diversity and inclusion. It especially reflects our experiences with the hundreds of mentors and mentees and multinational clients we work with at the Center for Mentoring Excellence.

This Book Is for You

This book is, of course, for mentors and mentees, both novices and experts. It is also for learning and development professionals, and anyone involved in leading, supervising, or managing the mentoring and diversity process in an organization. We have designed the examples and framework to stimulate your thinking about mentoring relationships and to encourage you to reflect deeply on your experiences. In addition, we've included a variety of practical tips and suggestions to promote more culturally aware engagement, cultural competency, and authenticity—all essential for supporting positive productive partnerships and better mentoring.

If you are a mentoring program manager, a diversity and inclusion leader, a learning professional, or an organizational leader or talent manager, we invite you to use this book as a guide to grow your leaders' cultural competency and elevate their mentoring practice. You will be better positioned to assist professionals engaged in mentoring management, coaching, troubleshooting, and developing internal communications about the mentoring program. Ultimately, regardless of your position in the organization, your understanding of cultural competency will benefit everyone. Learning how to communicate across differences will help you and your organization create a more inclusive workplace environment, bridge the gap between and among cultures, create cultural change, and make the most of your organization's investment in mentoring.

How to Use This Book

Above all, begin at the beginning. As tempting as it may be to skip over things you think you already know about yourself, we have found that there are no shortcuts to building bridges for better mentoring. The chapters in this book are divided into three primary sections:

Part 1. Lean Forward into Differences: This section is about *preparing yourself* for mentoring. These chapters are designed to help you understand cultural competency and increase self-understanding and skill at seeing differences. The exercises included in this section will help you increase your self-awareness and prepare you to recognize, acknowledge, and bridge differences in your mentoring relationship.

Part 2. Learn from Differences: Once you have prepared yourself for mentoring, you are ready to *prepare your relationship* with your mentoring partner. We will guide you through ways to learn more about each other—your commonalities and differences, worldviews, goals for the future, and more—and how to negotiate your differences to communicate effectively.

Part 3. Leverage Differences: The chapters in this section explore establishing agreements with your mentoring partner, goal setting, and goal achievement. You and your mentoring partner can use the tools in this section to enhance your learning by setting up your relationship in a way that acknowledges your differences and customizes the learning and the growth in a way that meets your needs and adapts to your differences.

This is not a workbook, but it does provide space for reflection. It is not a textbook, but it does offer practice-based guidance built on theory. Readily accessible, understandable, and relatable tools, practical strategies, and fictional mentoring narratives illustrate how the key concepts we discuss can play out in real-life mentoring contexts. In each chapter you will find brief "Your Turn" exercises to help you articulate and apply the principles in this book. Use them to reflect individually, to stimulate conversation and exploration with your mentoring partner, and to deepen your conversation and understanding. "Chapter Recaps" summarize key learning points at the end of each chapter. Both the Your Turn exercises and the Chapter Recaps facilitate understanding and retention of the ideas and concepts presented in this book.

We hope that *Bridging Differences* will help you see yourself, your mentoring partners, and the many people who contribute to your organization in a new and deeper way.

Why Bridging Differences Matters

We each bring who we are to our mentoring relationships. Yet "who we are" is composed of several elements: the person we see ourselves as, the person our mentoring partners see us as, and the unique cultural lens through which we view the world and the way it works. "Who we are" is determined by the many factors that shape our identity, culture, and worldview.

Unless you are working in a highly homogeneous organization, you will encounter visible and not-so-visible differences between who you are and who your mentoring partner is. The potential minefields for mentoring relationships are everywhere if we fail to adequately acknowledge and explore those differences in a way that promotes learning and satisfaction for both partners. Recognizing, understanding, and bridging these differences is crucial to a successful mentoring relationship. So often, we see "difference" not as belonging to us but to someone else. When we call someone "different," that makes us "normal." When each of us sees the other as "different," it pushes us apart and disconnects us. The truth is that there *is* no normal. Our differences rest *between* us, not within us. And because of this, the title of this book, *Bridging Differences*, is meant quite literally:

» A bridge is a structure that connects two distinct things.

» A bridge requires a solid foundation in order to stand securely.

» A bridge requires work, time, strategy, and focus to build.

» Building a bridge requires the help of other people. It is an active process involving connections, bonding, and collaboration; working together, we build a newer and richer mutual understanding.

When we don't understand the need to bridge the differences between us, we miss out on the richness those differences can bring to our relationships and we significantly limit the impact of our mentoring. What's more, if we don't take the time to build the skills needed to bridge these differences, we create conflict and misunderstanding, widening gaps instead of narrowing them. When we understand how to bridge differences, our mentoring relationships are better, our outcomes are better, and our organizations benefit from the differences between us. This benefit is clear, and it has caught the attention of growing numbers of employers. Increasingly, organizations are redefining mentorship to advance diversity and inclusion—and for good reason: diversity increases successful outcomes and grows the bottom line. According to a recent article in the *Wall Street Journal*, "Organizations with inclusive cultures are six times more likely to be innovative and agile, eight times more likely to achieve better business outcomes, and twice as likely to meet or exceed financial targets."[2]

Organizations with inclusive cultures actively pursue cultural competency—the skill that enables effective understanding and communication across the differences inherent in a diverse group of people. When cultural competency informs mentoring, learning is elevated, engagement and communication are enhanced, achievement of learning goals is accelerated, and relationships deepen. Whether you are a mentor or a mentee, bridging the differences between you and your partner—leaning forward into difference, learning from it, and leveraging it—allows you both to experience the promise and full potential of mentoring.

PART I

LEAN FORWARD *into* DIFFERENCES

Meet Mia and Christopher

At age thirty-five, Mia had been an associate at Farmer, French and Fowler LLP (F3) for five years. As far as Mia was concerned, her becoming partner couldn't happen fast enough. After graduating magna cum laude from college, she had worked as an executive recruiter for four years to save as much money as she could before applying to law school. She excelled in law school and fielded offers from top law firms across the country.

Of all the firms she interviewed with, F3 offered the best opportunity to build a labor and employment (L&E) practice. Its L&E practice was indisputably among the best in the United States. She was excited by the chance to work with top-tier clients as well as the possibility that she could work in any of the firm's twenty-three offices around the globe.

Mia had spirit and drive and boundless enthusiasm. She had success written all over her. She knew it and everyone around her knew it—including Christopher, her mentor. Mia was grateful that she had been assigned Christopher, a highly respected senior partner with a large book of business, and was looking forward to working with him. She was counting on him to help her shape her career and figure out what she needed to do to position herself to become an F3 partner when she became eligible in a few years.

Christopher grew up in Amsterdam, in the Netherlands, and had a short but successful career in international business before moving to New York in his early thirties. He'd earned his JD/MBA at Columbia University and come to F3 upon his graduation from law school. He quickly earned a reputation as a great litigator and, due to his business connections and easy nature, he moved steadily up the ladder. Now, at fifty-eight, he was confident, comfortable, and very successful.

When Christopher learned that Mia had been assigned to be his mentee, he was pleased, but he did have some reservations. He didn't know her well, but he was aware that she was smart, a go-getter, and always dressed for success. Christopher hadn't mentored a woman before, but his two grown daughters' experiences and activism in the #MeToo movement had made him particularly sensitive to gender issues, and he wondered if Mia might have been better paired with one of the firm's female partners instead.

Christopher checked in with Casey, F3's managing partner. "Why Mia?" he asked. Casey explained that the matches had all been made based on learning fit. Mia had the grit and potential to become a superstar. The team felt that the skills, knowledge, and relationships she needed to build aligned perfectly with Christopher's skills, knowledge, and experience. Christopher was still feeling a bit out of his element as he saw her walking toward his office for their first meeting. "Right on time—that's a good start," he thought, and breathed a little easier.

ONE

Building the Framework for Mentoring across Differences

When Mia and Christopher met for the first time, they were immediately struck by the ways in which they were not alike: gender, age, self-expression, and power differential within the organization. You will likely observe substantial differences between you and your mentoring partner. Some things (like ethnicity, race, and gender) may be easy to see; and some things (like values, motivation, and background) are not so visible. Often, we make unconscious assumptions about the meaning of what we see, and those assumptions may be incorrect because ethnicity, race, and gender are not always obvious and don't always follow an archetype. Nonetheless, each element of identity, and the assumptions that we make about them, affect how we view the world and how we view our mentoring partner.

When mentoring partners focus too much on differences, or when they can't relate across the differences, the result is fragmentation and judgment. Although it is tempting, and perhaps more comfortable, to focus on what we have in common with someone else, this can discourage authenticity, exclude the things you may learn if you pay attention to differences, and lead to other problems. The first question most people ask themselves when seeking to connect with a new person is, "What do we have in common?" In general, people connect based on commonality, which can give ground to build relationships. But when we are so focused on commonality, differences are ignored or even judged. Unconsciously, we create groupthink; and those who do not share the group's commonalities feel devalued, excluded, and discouraged from sharing differing ideas and opinions. Often, those of us who are excluding, however inadvertently, have no idea this is happening.

A multiplicity of factors make up our identity, shape the way we look at things, and impact our actions and our behavior. In mentoring (and in life in general), the idea is not to accentuate, avoid, or judge the ways we are different from one another but to *honor* those differences by balancing commonalities and differences. When we understand and appreciate the differences between us, we can leverage them to improve our conversations, deepen our learning, and spur creative thinking. When we see our partners through the lens of cultural competency, we enhance the relationship between mentor and mentee and boost mentoring outcomes.

What Is Mentoring?

We define mentoring as "a reciprocal learning relationship in which a mentor and mentee agree to a partnership where they work collaboratively toward achievement of mutually defined goals that will develop a mentee's skills, abilities, knowledge and/or thinking." This description is packed with a good deal of meaning for our work here. We focus on four key concepts that relate most closely to bridging difference in a mentoring relationship: *reciprocal, learning, relationship*, and *partnership*.

Mentoring Is Reciprocal

One of the most beneficial aspects of mentoring is its inherent reciprocity. When reciprocity is present, both mentor and mentee fully *engage* in the relationship. If the relationship is truly working, there is a big payoff for *both* parties. Perspectives expand, and each person gains new insight into where their mentoring partner is coming from. Each has specific responsibilities, contributes to the relationship, and learns from the other. Reciprocity is essential to effective mentoring, and the degree to which mentors mutually benefit from it is often surprising to both mentoring partners.

Mentoring Involves Learning

Mentoring, at its very core, is a learning relationship: learning is the purpose, the process, and the product of a mentoring relationship.[3] Mentees must come to the relationship as learners, and mentors must view themselves as learning facilitators and as learners. When both partners have a learning mindset, there is no failure. Rather, each encounter with difference and misunderstanding is an opportunity to learn from one another, to course correct and build on our new understandings. When mentors are open to learning, they often learn as much as (if not more than) their mentees.

Mentoring Requires a Strong Relationship

Effective mentoring requires a strong relationship between mentoring partners. From the very start, mentor and mentee must begin to build a relationship that is open and trusting and to honor each other's uniqueness. This doesn't happen overnight. Give your relationship time to develop and grow. It is the mentor's responsibility to create a safe and trusting space that enables a mentee to stretch and step outside their comfort zone, take risks, and show up authentically. It is the mentee's responsibility to be willing to take these risks, engage with their mentor, and ask for what they need. Both partners need to work at establishing, maintaining, and strengthening the relationship through time.

Mentoring Is a Partnership

Even though the mentor may be higher on the org chart than the mentee, a mentoring relationship is a partnership. Mentoring partners need to establish agreements that are anchored in a bedrock of trust. Trust is predicated on respecting your mentoring partner for who they are and understanding their needs. You are going to need to continuously work at building and strengthening your relationship and holding each other accountable for results. That is what strong partnerships do, and they do it well.

Mentoring is always a collaborative endeavor. Mentor and mentee work together to establish a successful relationship, achieve the mentee's goals, and make mentoring a win-win for both partners. Together they build the relationship, share knowledge, and come to consensus about the focus of the mentee's desired learning, and they actively engage with one another to achieve it.[4]

The Mentoring Cycle

Mentoring relationships travel through a predictable four-phase cycle, each building on the one before it to create a fluid developmental sequence: preparing, negotiating, enabling growth, and coming to closure. Being able to anticipate each phase, knowing where you are in the process, and understanding what each phase offers in terms of learning and growing with your mentoring partner, makes your

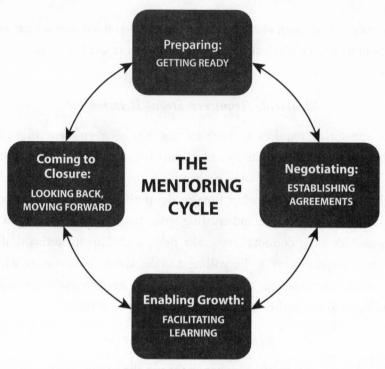

FIGURE 1.1   The Mentoring Cycle

work together more productive and builds a strong foundation for your partnership to succeed. This mentoring framework, which Lois presented in *The Mentor's Guide,* combines good mentoring practice with what we know about how adults learn best.[5]

Figure 1.1 shows the four phases of the mentoring cycle. We refer to these phases throughout this book. *There is no set time for getting through this cycle;* the length of each phase varies depending on the mentoring relationship. The two-way arrows between each phase indicate that the phases are fluid: mentoring partners sometimes need to revisit an earlier phase in the cycle in order to move forward. In this chapter we follow Christopher and Mia's journey as they begin phase 1 of their mentoring partnership.[6]

In the hundreds of conversations we've held with mentors and mentees, we've found that successful partnerships—those that can point to significant learning or progress—take care to follow these phases, often revisiting steps as needs and goals change.[7] Positive movement through each phase rests on successful completion of specific behaviors and processes. Have faith in the process and be patient.

Phase 1. Preparing

Preparing has two parts: preparing yourself as mentor or mentee and then preparing the relationship. Preparing yourself is critical, yet it is frequently overlooked. Most folks just step into mentoring and gear up when they first meet their mentoring partner. Maybe they look over their partner's CV and get some background info about the person. But just as you might get your thoughts together before making a presentation, the better way to mentor is to *prepare yourself* before you engage in your mentoring relationship.

The second part of preparing—*preparing the relationship*—focuses on the kickoff conversation you engage in with your mentoring partner. Mia and Christopher, whom you met earlier, are just embarking on their mentoring relationship. They haven't scratched the surface of it yet, let alone begun to bridge differences. What you read in the mentoring story before this chapter represents everything Mia and Christopher know about each other, and it's the tip of the iceberg—gender, level of professional experience, job title, and age. What they do not yet know still lies beneath the surface: their unique motivations and expectations. They have work to do to get to know each other beyond what they see at first glance, and this work will lay the foundation for a trusting relationship that encourages authenticity.

Both Christopher and Mia need to explore and discover the other person as an individual. What do they care about? What motivates them? What is their view of work and authority? What has their personal journey been? The purpose of this phase is to work toward creating a fuller understanding about who your mentoring partner is: What makes up the "who" of this unique individual? Getting to know another person and reaching a deeper level of understanding doesn't happen in one meeting. It is a process that unfolds gradually and relies on a high degree of trust that takes time to build. With trust comes increased comfort. The more comfortable one is, the more open one can be; the more open one can be, the more authentic the conversation. The more authentic mentors and mentees are with each other, the deeper and more effective the learning.

Mia and Christopher's first meeting was typical of many relationships. Although both partners felt like they knew what they needed to accomplish, and felt prepared to succeed, neither had prepared themselves in a way that would build trust and understanding.

Mia was excited and impatient to get started—she felt more than ready for her meeting. She arrived in Christopher's office with three lists: the goals she was ready to work on, the matters she had worked on since she joined F3, and the partners who had a book of business she admired. After a few minutes of getting acquainted, Mia handed her lists to Christopher. "This is what I want to work on," she said. "What's my next best step?"

Christopher was taken aback. He was impressed with Mia's organization and drive, but to him, she appeared to be moving way too fast. "Seems a bit soon to dive into that," he said, handing back her lists after a brief glance. "I need to understand more about you and how you work best." Christopher smiled at Mia, but he felt like a tornado had just burst through his door.

Disappointed and annoyed, Mia took back her papers. She was too busy for this. Making time for mentoring meetings was actually taking up time she could be spending on work, and she just wanted to get moving. How long could this take, anyway? And why didn't Christopher take her at her word that she knew what she wanted to work on? He seemed too dismissive of the goals and the lists she had spent so much time crafting. She wondered if she should just cut her losses and find another mentor.

As your mentoring partnership unfolds, trust is built and your relationship grows. The information you need about one another reveals itself over time.

Phase 2. Negotiating

Negotiating is the "business" phase of the relationship. Taking time to set processes and structures in place that you both agree on helps ensure mentoring success. Negotiating the parameters of your mentoring relationship involves conversations about goals, processes, ground rules, timelines, and accountabilities. When well executed, negotiating builds a rock-solid foundation for moving forward and staying on track, but it cannot be accomplished without first understanding who your mentoring partner is. Otherwise, mentoring becomes formulaic; better mentoring is not one-size-fits-all.

At their next meeting, Mia walked into Christopher's office with a pen and a notebook—no lists this time. She felt a real urgency to get to work on her list of goals. Though she was still annoyed about their last meeting, she was also pragmatic. This was a great opportunity for her to connect with an influential colleague who probably did have something to teach her. She didn't want to alienate Christopher, so she decided to try his approach.

Christopher was ready for another onslaught when Mia walked in, but he was delighted to see Mia's notebook and no lists. She seemed ready to listen. So, after some small talk, he began. "Let's set some ground rules," he said.

Mia sighed to herself. She was ready to work! Why did he want to drag this on? "I'd better buckle up," she thought, "this is going to be a long ride."

Phase 3. Enabling Growth

Phase 3, enabling growth, is the longest phase of the mentoring relationship. Now the work of mentoring begins in earnest, as you and your mentoring partner dive into goal achievement. This is where you will spend most of your time, so you want to do a good job of preparing the relationship to keep it growing, keep the learning fresh, and move forward toward achieving your mutual goals.

Mentoring relationships often stall out during this phase, so mutual accountability is paramount. Frequent check-ins will allow for course correction on the process, the goal, and the relationship. During this phase the mentor is supporting, challenging, and encouraging the mentee to create and articulate a vision of possibility. The mentee needs to be able to ask for what they need, and feedback conversations are the norm.

After a few more meetings, Christopher and Mia settled on two goals for Mia. The first one was straightforward: by the end of the mentoring year, she would identify ten potential clients or referral sources and build relationships with the key players. The second goal, however, was a bit tougher. Because Mia was so focused on becoming a partner, she would need to become more aware of how she presented herself so that others saw her potential.

From the start, Christopher knew that Mia needed to learn to speak more slowly and moderately. But telling her to slow down and encouraging her to realize that her speedy approach was holding her back was another matter altogether. Mia's energy was a positive attribute, her verbal attack mode less so. Christopher wanted Mia to show up authentically, and he anticipated that this would be a sensitive subject. Experience had taught him that telling Mia to slow down was only going to put her on the defensive, so he decided to put the ball in her court.

Christopher asked Mia questions about how she thought she was viewed in the firm.

She seemed puzzled by the query. "I've never thought about it," Mia said. "I'm really not sure...is this important?"

"Well," Christopher replied slowly, "I've learned that when I know how clients and colleagues see me, it helps me know how to approach them and better get my points across." Therefore, the second goal they set was more long-term and personal: over the next six months, Mia would work on increasing her self-awareness so that she understood how she was perceived by her fellow attorneys and potential clients.

Mia was taken aback—six months of wasting time on "getting to know herself"? This wasn't therapy! But on reflection, and despite her initial suspicions, she thought that it might be an interesting learning experience. Still, she found herself annoyed and confused by her mentor's motives. Did Christopher really respect her? What was she doing that even made him say that? She wondered if it was a male-female thing. Maybe a woman partner would have been better after all, Mia mused.

Phase 4. Coming to Closure

In the fourth phase, mentor and mentee focus on consolidating and integrating the learning, evaluating the learning, celebrating the learning, and moving on. This short phase actually offers the most opportunity for growth and reflection, regardless of whether the relationship has been positive or not. Good closure conversation acts as a rite of passage, offering a framework for moving on and opening the door to new development opportunities. Closure provides an opportunity to reflect on what you've learned, process it, and talk about how you are going to leverage and take your learning to the next level.

Phase 4 is not a one-time-only offer. Mia and Christopher will circle back through this phase several times if they continue to be mentor and mentee for the long haul. Successful closure creates new opportunities for growth. If closure is to be a mutually satisfying learning experience, both partners must be prepared for it. A closure conversation is one of the most significant development conversations you will ever have as a mentor or mentee, so take every opportunity to maximize the experience. (As you'll learn later in this book, closure doesn't necessarily mean "the end." It's a good rule of thumb never to bring a mentoring relationship to closure without identifying the next growth goal.)

» YOUR TURN «

1. Think about your mentoring experiences. In what ways were any of the four concepts (partnership, strong relationship, learning, reciprocity) present? In what ways were they missing?

_____

_____

_____

_____

2. Reflect on your past mentoring experiences. Might a more structured model have helped make them more successful? In what ways?

_____

_____

_____

_____

The mentoring concepts laid out in this chapter are basic to the mentoring process. In the next chapter you'll begin to build the foundation for allowing cultural competency to inform your mentoring partnerships.

Chapter Recap

1. The ideal mentoring relationship is a cycle comprised of four phases: preparing, negotiating, enabling growth, and coming to closure. Completion of each phase is critical to a successful mentoring relationship.

2. Mentoring pairs can move backward and forward between the phases, but skipping a phase will deprive each partner of the full benefit of mentoring.

3. Mentoring is a collaborative, reciprocal partnership that focuses on mutually defined goals for the mentee's learning and development. It is cocreated by the mentor and mentee and customized based on each pair's needs and preferences.

4. Mentoring partners can connect based on what they have in common and based upon their differences. Pairs need not view differences as obstacles to connection. The key is to understand differences and use them as ways to connect with one another.

TWO

Seeing the Differences between Us

We often meet someone and think they are "different" but people are not inherently different: our differences lie *between* us, not within us. We believe that leaning forward into the differences between people, learning from those differences, and leveraging them creates stronger relationships. It is in this space that the magic of mentoring happens.

What Do Diversity, Inclusion, and Cultural Competency Really Mean?

We often hear the words "diversity," "inclusion," and "cultural competency," but people may understand them differently. Before we go deeper, let's agree on some definitions.

Diversity

Diversity means *difference*. Even if everyone in your organization presents in a similar way on the surface—race, gender, ethnicity, age—diversity is a reality. It is vital to keep in mind that the many people we meet every day, even if they look like us, bring their own unique perspectives and backgrounds that may be far different from what we assume.

Though many organizations rightly focus on visible differences (gender, age, race, ethnicity, differing abilities, for example), diversity also includes nonvisible differences in identity (such as sexual orientation, religion, gender identity). But there are myriad other differences as well: in experience (family status, life experiences, social class, education), beliefs (such as political beliefs), in skill and knowledge (in hard skills and so-called soft-skills, like emotional intelligence), and personality elements (such as introversion or extroversion, and communication style). In mentoring, diversity answers the question "*Who* is in your mentoring relationship?" The *who* includes the unique mix of human differences—ethnicity, gender, gender identity, sexual orientation, age, social class, physical abilities/attributes, religion, national origin, political beliefs, race, life experiences—that make up each individual.

Inclusion

Inclusion is *how you respond to diversity in the workplace to make it meaningful*. Simply hiring a diverse mix of employees is meaningless unless each person is actively included as a respected and contributing member of the team. Studies have shown that teams that are diverse but not inclusive will underperform compared with monocultural teams, while teams that are both diverse *and* inclusive will outperform monocultural teams.[8] Andrés Tapia, a leading global thinker in diversity and inclusion, perhaps said it best: "Diversity is the mix and inclusion is making the mix work."[9]

In mentoring, "inclusion" means ensuring that both mentor and mentee feel valued, heard, and respected in the relationship. We effect inclusion through the skill of cultural competency.

Cultural Competency

Cultural competency is the skill we use to *effectively understand and communicate across differences*. Cultural competency is the *how*: the path to achieving inclusion and the path to leveraging diversity, to making inclusion come to life. Without cultural competency, mentoring partners miss out on what could become a much more powerful and dynamic mentoring relationship. Mentoring that bridges differences promotes inclusion; it enables mentoring partners to feel comfortable being themselves and authentically expressing their thoughts and experiences. Like any skill, cultural competency requires practice to get better.

Cultural competency involves

» Recognizing that cultural differences are a fact of life.

» Seeing the world and the people you meet as different from yourself in ways you may not have considered.

» Seeing how your own culture, invisible to yourself, has had a profound impact on how you look at things. Cultural competency is *not* about abandoning your own cultural identity.

» Recognizing that cultural differences *do* make a difference in how we show up: how we greet one another, view authority, get motivated, and understand the world can vary greatly. Note, however, that cultural competency is *not* about doing endless research to understand specific customs of each culture in order to lessen your likelihood of inadvertently insulting or disrespecting your partner.

» Learning how to notice differences without judgment, and using that information to learn, adjust your approach if necessary, and achieve better outcomes and more meaningful relationships as a result.

» Getting curious enough about your own cultural identity to be able to notice differences and understand yourself in a way that helps you relate better across difference.

Bridging Differences 1-2-3

Sociologist Milton Bennett, the creator of the Developmental Model of Intercultural Sensitivity, says that bridging difference is about adaptation, not assimilation. "It is additive, not substitutive."[10] That is, cultural competency allows us to shift and expand our perspective, not to limit it, change it, or turn it into something else. Creating meaningful mentoring relationships means taking the time and making the space to become aware of difference, to understand that difference, and to invite it into the relationship. To successfully bridge differences requires moving through three steps: taking ownership, creating awareness, and shifting perspective.

Step 1. Take Ownership

Taking ownership of your own responsibility to bridge differences—regardless of what your mentoring partner is doing—is where mentoring begins. This means recognizing that it is up to you to work on your own ability to communicate across difference. It also means recognizing that you might benefit from a broader perspective by acknowledging when differences appear and taking steps to invite those differences in so that they can improve your relationships and outcomes.

Taking ownership has two essential elements: (1) getting curious and (2) adopting a growth mindset. The authors of the *Harvard Business Review* article "From Curious to Competent" define curiosity as "a penchant for seeking new experiences, knowledge, and feedback and an openness to change."[11] In the context of mentoring, curiosity means being willing to gain knowledge and awareness of both your own identity, thoughts, and motivations and those of your mentoring partner. Curiosity is about constantly asking open questions that invite discussion and feedback, such as "How might you see this differently than I do?" and "What am I missing?"

In her book *Mindset: The New Psychology of Success,* researcher Carol Dweck explains that we can have either a fixed mindset or a growth mindset when it comes to certain skills or behaviors we wish to develop. A fixed mindset is one in which people believe that their basic qualities (such as their intelligence, talent, and knowledge) are fixed traits. In mentoring, a fixed mindset would show up as "My mentoring partner and I are so different. I just don't understand where he is coming from." In contrast, a growth mindset is one in which people believe that their most basic abilities can be developed through dedication, hard work, and learning. In the context of mentoring, a growth mindset would show up as "I can tell that my mentoring partner sees things differently. I don't understand it, but I want to learn more about it."

A growth mindset allows mentors and mentees to learn more about how difference shows up, to create understanding and an appreciation of differing viewpoints. Developing a growth mindset is not a diversion from the learning. Rather, it is an essential step to deepen and accelerate the learning.

Step 2. Create Awareness

Once we've taken ownership, we can begin to cultivate first self-awareness and then awareness of others. The latter (awareness of others) cannot exist without the former (awareness of self). Industrial designer Charles Eames wrote: "The details are not the details, they make the design." So often, particularly in the work context, we are tempted to skip over the details—the "getting to know you" part of the relationship—and "just get to the work." In mentoring, the getting to know you part *is* the first step of the work. And it starts with understanding your own cultural lens.

Early in coauthor Lisa's career, as she was balancing a long workweek and two very young children, a male coworker said to her, "I don't see you as a working mother." Though the comment was meant by the coworker to convey that he saw Lisa as an equal member of the team, to Lisa, for whom so much of her identity was centered on balancing work and motherhood, it felt that she wasn't being seen. If we don't *see* the details—that is, the elements of one another's identities that shape our worldviews—we are likely to miss opportunities to relate authentically with one another.

Awareness *must* begin with understanding yourself. Many prospective and current mentors and mentees skip over this step, assuming that, as functioning adults, they know themselves well. Yet, even though understanding oneself is the threshold step to creating meaningful personal and work relationships, few adults seem to have taken the time to think about what their own motivators and assumptions are, and how their identity and experiences have shaped how they show up and interact with others. (Later in this book we provide some tools and tips for you to create a greater sense of self-awareness. The exercise at the end of this chapter will get you started.)

Once you have created greater self-awareness, you can become more aware of your mentoring partner and start to get curious about ways your perspectives, motivations, or assumptions may be similar or different. This helps both of you communicate better, create more durable goals, and set a foundation for the relationship that will spur deeper learning and more measurable results. Focusing on self-awareness helps us become aware of our biases and surface our unconscious biases. Unconscious bias is influenced by our deeply held beliefs, past experiences, and cultural conditioning, and always affects our thinking and decisions. Unconscious bias gets triggered when our brain makes quick judgments and assessments about people and situations.

Taking ownership requires accepting that we have biases, acknowledging those biases, and then learning how to mitigate them. Our biases are related to many things. They include more obvious elements of identity like race and gender, and less obvious things like political orientation, speech patterns, geography, and socioeconomic status. Let's see how acknowledging bias plays out in Christopher and Mia's initial meetings.

Early on, Christopher realized that he had an innate bias against Mia's rapid-fire way of talking. He had been brought up in a household where people expressed themselves more slowly and thoughtfully, and he experienced her as intrusive, careless, and perhaps disrespectful. Christopher thought this aspect of Mia's presentation might alienate others beside himself, but he did not want to insult her by mentioning it head on. Instead, he asked her to observe how people experienced her. After a few weeks of getting to know Mia, Christopher realized that his initial knee-jerk bias against how she spoke had actually prevented him from listening to what she was saying.

Acknowledging a bias is not an admission that you are a bad person. It is, however, a necessary factor in creating awareness and overcoming the biases so that you can build bridges in your mentoring and other relationships. Bringing the unconscious to consciousness depends on a real commitment to self-awareness and an ongoing openness to noticing our behaviors and assumptions. Once that happens, you can move on to the third essential step, perspective shifting. This is not easy, but it is essential.

Step 3. Shift Your Perspective

According to author Dr. Wayne Dyer, "When you change the way you look at things, the things you look at change."[12] While cultural competency requires the willingness to see things differently, it does not mean compromising your authenticity or adopting alternative viewpoints. Rather, it means noticing and being curious about other perspectives, and being willing to consider and reconsider your own assumptions when you learn new information about yourself or others. Cultural competency bridges differences by expanding your knowledge and perspective.

Cultural competency is particularly important in mentoring relationships because learning and growth are at the heart of the relationship for both the mentee *and* the mentor. The way we learn, motivate others to learn, and show up to learn is dependent on our identities, which are influenced by our own backgrounds, preferences, and experiences. In a mentoring relationship, there are at least two distinct perspectives: that of the mentee and that of the mentor. If we do not notice, get curious, and seek to understand these distinctions, we risk missing valuable insight and squander the opportunity to create meaningful goals that motivate, inspire, and sustain a healthy and vibrant mentoring relationship.

Why We Need Cultural Competency

As research shows, we instinctively tend to seek out people who look like us.[13] Sameness can be a shortcut for comfort and creates a sense of ease, but it sometimes encourages us to avoid the hard work of understanding difference. When we surround ourselves in sameness, we miss out on a tremendous opportunity to learn, and we prevent ourselves from expanding our perspectives. When most of our interactions are with people whom we believe are like us, we tend to assume *everyone* is like us, which precludes us from practicing the curiosity and awareness essential to creating meaningful relationships with those who are in fact different from us. In her autobiography *Becoming,* former US first lady Michelle Obama reminds us that "sameness breeds more sameness until you make a thoughtful effort to counteract it."[14]

Mastering the skill of cultural competency is essential to better mentoring and deeper learning. When mentoring partners bridge their differences, they build inclusion and understanding. When they exercise their skills of cultural competency, they encourage authenticity and sharing, and are better able to craft learning solutions and witness the exponential growth that effective mentoring can create. Better mentoring can be a catalyst to creating more inclusive workplaces. Inclusive policies, systemic programming, and leadership buy-in are certainly important to creating change. But there is no substitute to creating meaningful workplace relationships across differences, and they have at least two major benefits: they enable both people in a relationship to feel seen, heard, and valued for who they are, and they increase the learning and perspective of both people in the relationship. One-to-one relationships require approaching difference with the development and demonstration of curiosity, awareness, and willingness to learn.

Effective mentoring encourages people to show up authentically. Significantly, learning how to bridge differences in mentoring translates into more competent leaders who invite difference into the workplace. This raises the level of engagement and performance in the teams and departments they lead. The level of interaction that mentoring demands, paired with the vulnerability and inquisitiveness that culturally competent individuals demand, is a powerful combination that leverages the benefits of mentoring, inclusion, and strong leadership.

As you take time to become more self-aware, you'll begin to notice less obvious differences between yourself and others. For mentors, this understanding helps you recognize when and how you can motivate and encourage your mentee. For mentees, this understanding fosters recognition of how to best communicate with your mentor. Consider Mia's journey toward creating more self-awareness.

When Mia first began exploring her goal of looking at how others saw her, she actually started paying more attention to how others presented themselves. She noticed that Christopher generally paused a moment before replying to her questions or comments. Initially, it drove her crazy—she wanted to make the most of their time together and his pause made her impatient. But then she realized that this pause also gave her the impression that he was thinking about what she said. Mia started to wonder if her habit of speaking quickly was coming off as not paying attention. She began to adjust the speed of her speech in their mentoring meetings and noticed that Christopher seemed to be unconsciously speeding up a bit in his responses. She concluded that somehow they were beginning to understand each other a little better.

Creating self-awareness coincides with the preparation phase of mentoring, preparing you to increase both your cultural competency and your effectiveness as a mentoring partner. Whether you are a mentor or a mentee, preparing yourself for mentoring is going to be key to your success. It requires self-awareness, a growth mindset, and a readiness to learn.

Start with Self-Awareness

Self-awareness is fundamental to the success of both mentors and mentees, and reflection kick-starts the process. Reflecting means letting go of preconceptions and trusting yourself enough to intentionally, honestly, and openly explore your motivation for engaging in mentoring. This will not be time wasted.

Coauthor Lois has written that reflection—"the ability to critically examine your current or past practices, behaviors, actions and thoughts in order to more consciously and purposefully develop yourself personally and professionally"—is an instrumental part of mentoring.[15] You will find, as many mentors and mentees do, that time spent on self-awareness will enrich more than just your mentoring; it will help you gain perspective and access tools to enhance your work and personal relationships as well. Through reflection, Mia gleaned several key insights.

Mia had always considered herself pretty self-aware, but she found herself unable to answer some of Christopher's questions about what motivated her. And although she knew she wanted to become partner, she couldn't really explain why, or what kind of leader she wanted to become. She realized that she wasn't nearly as self-aware as she had thought, and she would need to think more about her motivation so that she and Christopher could move forward.

It is hard to overstate the potential transformative power of self-reflection. Yet when we suggest to new mentors or mentees that they take time for self-awareness, we tend to hear one or both of these objections: "I already know myself pretty well" or "In the name of efficiency, let's just dive in and we'll get to know each other along the way." Reflection may not seem very important, but it is critical for success and can be powerful. It allows you to combine hindsight, insight, and foresight in a way that catapults you forward into action.[16]

"I Already Know Myself Pretty Well"

Understanding yourself generally and understanding yourself in the context of difference are not the same thing. In our experience we find that even the most senior leaders—in fact, *especially* the most senior leaders—know what works for them in their environment; but they don't always understand how that might be different for others, or how their own identity shapes their comfort in their current environment.

This is particularly true for individuals who are in the majority culture in which they work. It is sometimes said that a fish in water doesn't know it is wet. If we happen to be in a majority culture, it can be difficult to realize the limits of our perspective that are easily seen and felt by others *not* in our group. If we operate in an environment of familiarity, we rarely take the time to think about what makes us comfortable in that environment, or how it might be different for others. The Greek philosopher Epictetus said that it is impossible for us to learn what we think we already know. The key to becoming self-aware is to realize that there is a lot that we don't yet know about ourselves, and to consciously set an intention to learn more. Taking ownership of the responsibility to learn about difference requires a growth mindset: realizing that we all have an ability to learn, grow, and see things from a different perspective.

Individuals engaged in successful mentoring relationships commit to learning from each other. They are intensely curious. They constantly ask questions. They continually reflect on their experiences, both positive and negative. A growth mindset means that you believe in yourself and own the power of your own possibilities, and it also means that you also possess faith in the power of possibility that learning through difference presents. It can feel inefficient to take the time for self-reflection before beginning a mentoring relationship. And yet, without this investment in time, when mentees or mentors encounter significant differences between themselves and their mentoring partners, they tend either to miss or gloss over those differences altogether. Worse, you might find yourself feeling stuck when confronted with these differences because you don't know how to bridge them.

Taking the time for self-awareness helps in creating awareness of your mentoring partner and allows you both to create a deeper more authentic mentoring relationship. Investing the time upfront helps you go farther and faster when you meet these differences in any context. In the increasingly diverse workforce, you will inevitably encounter differences in your working relationships, if not in your mentoring relationship.

» YOUR TURN «

1. When it comes to bridging differences, what are your strengths?

_____

_____

_____

_____

2. In thinking about the characteristics of a growth mindset, where are your opportunities for development?

_____

_____

_____

_____

Leaning forward into differences means accepting that you might not yet completely understand how and why differences matter, that you can indeed learn about differences, that you can understand your own identity and biases (and perhaps privilege), and that there is value in doing so. In short, it requires ownership and self-awareness. It requires that you identify aspects of your mindset so that you see how your mindset may be inhibiting you from creating meaningful connections across difference.

With awareness, you can begin to replace your limiting beliefs with those that will enable you to increase your cultural competency. In the context of difference, self-awareness is about exploring our culture, identity, biases, and privilege—a process we begin in the next chapter.

Chapter Recap

1. It is essential to get comfortable with reflecting (on your own attitudes and the world around you) if you are going to be an authentic mentoring partner. You need to know yourself in order to truly begin to know someone else.

2. Approaching differences with curiosity instead of judgment requires a growth mindset. Having a growth mindset will help you make the most of mentoring, keeping you open to the possibility that you can learn more about differences without compromising your sense of self.

3. Awareness of differences is the key to bridging differences, and the first step in this process is self-awareness. *Even if you think you already know yourself well,* it is helpful to reflect on your own identity and culture so that you can be more aware of and understanding about the differences between you and your mentoring partner.

THREE

Culture and Identity in Mentoring

Culture lives in the collective. It is the combined customs, arts, social institutions, and achievements of a particular nation, people, or other social group and is reflected in the behavior, beliefs, and outlook of a group of people. *Identity* is individual, made up of who we are individually and how we see ourselves in the context of society and the world. Our own identity may draw from many cultures and may or may not reflect the archetypical beliefs that categorize the cultures with which we identify. Every individual interprets and adapts cultural influence differently. Exploring your identity requires looking at how your own culture has impacted you. So first, let's talk about culture.

Culture and Interpersonal Relationships

Most people associate culture with things like food, music, religious traditions, and celebrations. Indeed, these are reflections of culture, but there is much more that categorizes a culture than these objective elements. Each culture shares language, educational, philosophical, and religious systems, and values, laws, and unwritten rules of conduct that influence behavior, beliefs, and outlook.

In *Riding the Waves of Culture*, management experts Fons Trompenaars and Charles Hampden-Turner explain that "culture is the way in which a group of people solve problems and reconcile dilemmas."[17] They suggest five ways that different cultures address interpersonal relationships that we find particularly relevant to the framework we describe in this book.

1. Applying Rules:
Universalism and Particularism

Cultures that tend toward *universalism* approach problems as absolute and universally applicable (that is, the same rules apply to everyone). Cultures that tend toward *particularism* place far greater emphasis on relationships and unique circumstances (that is, different rules apply in different contexts). Imagine the judgment that someone at one end of the spectrum might apply to someone at the other end. A person who is universalistic might say of someone who is particularistic: "That person is shady. He won't hold his own brother to the same rules as everyone else." On the opposite end of the spectrum, someone who is particularistic might say: "That person is shady. He won't even bend the rules for his own brother!"

2. Role of the Group:
Individualism and Communitarianism

Individualist cultures focus first on individual contributions, while *communitarian* cultures focus on the community first. In a communitarian culture, individual achievement can often be perceived as selfish or disrespectful. In an individualistic culture, however, it is expected that one would first look after their own needs and then those of the community. In this case, someone who tempers their own achievement so as not to stick out from the crowd may be viewed as lazy, cowardly, or unduly passive.

3. Role of Emotions:
Neutral and Affective

A *neutral* culture places more value on being detached, objective, and unemotional. In an *affective* culture, lack of emotional expressiveness is seen as being too dispassionate, or even as uninterested. Neutral cultures view the expression of emotion as a weakness. Anger or intense emotions are viewed as unprofessional and signal a lack of objectivity. This attitude was made explicit in the famous line from the movie *A League of Their Own*: "There's no crying in baseball!" It is still the unspoken rule in mainstream US business culture (and in fact that line in itself is reflective of a culture clash). In affective cultures, however, expressing emotion is a sign that you are invested in the outcome and in the relationship. Lack of expressiveness can be viewed as a lack of interest.

4. Scope of Relationship:
Specific and Diffuse

Some cultures see relationships as limited to a *specific* topic (such as focusing only on work-related goals, common in mainstream US business culture), while other cultures are more *diffuse*, requiring a broader, whole-life perspective (such as how to balance work and life priorities). Trompenaars and Hampden-Turner explain that "doing business with a culture more diffuse than our own feels excessively time consuming....In diffuse cultures, everything is connected to everything. Your business partner may wish to know where you went to school, who your friends are, and what you think of life, politics, art, literature and music. This is not a waste of time, because such preferences reveal character and form friendships."[18]

5. How Accomplishment is Measured:
Achievement and Ascription

In cultures aligned with *achievement*, people are judged by what they have accomplished. In cultures aligned with *ascription*, people are judged by the status attached to certain aspects of their identity, who they are (family, age, birth, gender), by their connections, and by their educational record. "In an achievement culture," Trompenaars and Hampden-Turner explain, "the first question is likely to be '*What* did you study?' In a more ascriptive culture, the question will more likely be '*Where* did you study?'"[19]

» YOUR TURN «

1. Place an "✗" on each continuum where you see yourself on Table 3.1. Place a checkmark (✓) on each continuum where you see your culture of origin. Place an asterisk (✱) where you see your organizational culture. Then answer the questions that follow.

TABLE 3.1 *Where are you on each cultural continuum?*

Universalism	How we apply rules	Particularism
Same rules apply to everyone Rules trump relationship	O———O———O	Rules differ based on relationship Relationships trump rules

Individualism	Role of the group	Communitarianism
Focus on individual needs, goals, and objectives over group	O———O———O	Focus on group needs, goals, and objectives over individual

Neutral	Role of emotions	Affective
Control or suppress emotions	O———O———O	Express or demonstrate emotions

Specific	Scope of relationship	Diffuse
Workplace conversations limited to work issues or specific topic	O———O———O	Workplace conversations cover many aspects of life

Achievement	How accomplishment is measured	Ascription
Status derived from doing and achievement	O———O———O	Status derived from being, your attributes, and connections

Source: © 2019, Center for Mentoring Excellence

2. How do the factors you discovered in the continuum table affect your work relationships?

_____

_____

_____

_____

3. If there is a difference between where you see yourself and where you see your organizational culture, what impact does that difference have on your work life?

_____

_____

_____

_____

The Identity Iceberg

Your culture is an intricate combination of the environmental factors that shaped you, but your identity is *you:* the way you think about yourself, the way you are viewed by the world, your personality, and the characteristics that you and others choose to define you. Identity consists of both the simple facts about you (such as your name, where you live, your height and weight) and more complex elements (such as your culture, your gender identity, your motivation, your religious beliefs and values).

We like to think of identity as an iceberg: about 20 percent of our identity is visible to the world, and 80 percent of its substance is below the waterline, invisible at first glance. All the elements of our identity shape how we show up in the world, how we view the world, and how the world views us. For example, if Mia and Christopher were to complete their own icebergs, they might look like Figures 3.1 and 3.2.

When you think of the elements that make you *you*, you might think of things you can see, the visible 20 percent (gender expression, skin color, age, physical ability), or of things you can't see but which lay just beneath the surface (ethnicity, national origin, religion, socioeconomic status, sexual orientation, political beliefs, education level, and life experience). What you probably don't consider are two significant components of every individual's iceberg: what motivates you and what you value. These always lie below the waterline, sometimes so deep that we are not fully aware of how these factors impact us until we spend time reflecting on it. It is this reflection that is essential to preparing yourself for your mentoring relationship.

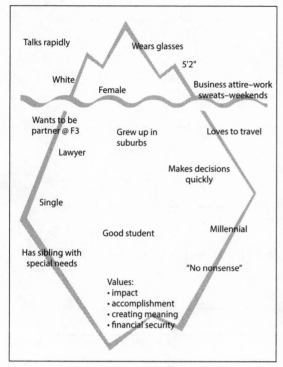

FIGURE 3.1 Mia's Iceberg

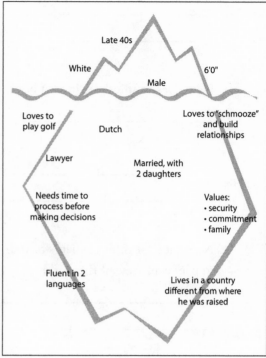

FIGURE 3.2 Christopher's Iceberg

» YOUR TURN «

Take the time to reflect on your own iceberg. Draw your iceberg if that makes it easier.

1. What elements of your identity are readily visible to other people?

    _____

    _____

    _____

    _____

2. How does your iceberg impact how you relate to others?

    _____

    _____

_____

_____

3. How does your iceberg impact how others relate to you?

_____

_____

_____

_____

4. Name at least three elements of your identity that people cannot see that impact your view of the world.

_____

_____

_____

_____

When we think of our identity, we often get stuck on the visible 20 percent and forget about other characteristics, styles, and preferences that influence us. Two key below-the-waterline factors that often influence mentoring relationships are *motivation* and *learning style*.

Motivation

In a mentoring relationship, it is essential to understand what motivates you to show up at work every day and what motivates you to participate in mentoring. You can determine this by reflecting on questions like: Why do I work? What *sort* of work do I hope to have? What impact do I hope to have on the organization and the people I work with?

Many studies have shown that the meaning people give to work and the drivers of employee engagement are similar across generations, yet the meaning that people give those factors varies by generation.[20] For example, although all generations seem to seek a sense of purpose in their work, baby boomers (born 1943–60) tend to focus on achieving an impact within the organization. In contrast, millennials (born 1981–2000) look for work that will help them achieve a sense of purpose in the greater social context. Building a career is a primary motivator for baby boomers and Gen Xers (born 1961–80), while millennials seek more to craft a life that integrates work with interests outside of work. Baby boomers are typically motivated by perks and public recognition.[21]

Gen Xers tend to value freedom and can be motivated by time to pursue other interests or have fun at work.[22] Millennials are typically motivated by the chance to make an impact, have a career path, and get feedback on their learning.[23] The postmillennial generation (sometimes referred to as Gen Z or iGen), those born after 2000, enter the workplace with an entrepreneurial and global mindset.[24] They are highly diverse and multicultural, therefore likely to actively seek learning opportunities such as mentoring for the sake of garnering more life experiences.[25]

What motivates someone depends on more than just their generation, of course; it varies by individual based on other factors as well. For example, we once met a young attorney who was passionate about her desire to help refugees and immigrants. After law school she went to work in a large law firm to get experience in complex cases and earn enough to pay down her law school loans. She intended to work in the firm five years and then parlay her skills to do legal work on behalf of immigrants and refugees in the public sector. She looked for a mentor at the firm but could not find one who seemed to understand that she did not want to become partner and wasn't motivated by the same things as her generational peers. Every time she approached a potential mentor, their guidance would be to learn how to develop a book of business or to position herself with influential partners who could help her develop client relationships. Yet this woman's motivation was not aligned with the guidance.

Take a few moments now to reflect on what motivates you.

» YOUR TURN «

1. What motivates you to show up for work each day?

_____

_____

_____

_____

2. When have you felt most motivated to set and achieve goals?

_____

_____

_____

_____

3. What is your vision for yourself in three years? Five years?

_____

_____

_____

_____

How Identity Impacts Motivation for Mentoring

Your motivation for being a mentor or mentee definitely impacts the mentoring relationship. There are many reasons why mentors choose to mentor and many reasons why mentees opt for mentoring. Mentors may have specific knowledge they want to pass on to others. They may find joy and reward in helping others learn, or they might want to pay it forward. Mentees may have their sights set on advancing in their organization, shifting their career path, or expanding their networks. Both mentors and mentees may get energized by learning from others different from themselves. They may see mentoring as a personal growth and development opportunity. They may want to mentor or be mentored by a specific person. Mentoring might be a performance requirement or leadership responsibility.

Christopher had recently become more attuned to how things were for women in the workplace, and he viewed mentoring as a chance to pay it forward for his two grown daughters. The two mentors whom you will meet in later chapters, Heather and Darren, were motivated for other reasons. Heather's motivation was to pave the way for the next generation of women leaders so that it would be easier for them to make their mark and achieve their potential. Darren viewed mentoring as part of his leadership responsibility. He was committed to strengthening the leadership bench in his organization.

Mentees' motivations also vary. They may come to mentoring through compliance to a performance requirement. They may be seeking to emulate a role model or desire to learn from someone with specific experience, expertise, or talent, as in Mia's case. Heather's mentee, Aesha, sought mentoring as a personal growth and development opportunity. Others may just enjoy the collaborative learning that results from mentoring; or they may want to develop a more global mindset. Mentees who identify with groups that are traditionally underrepresented in the workplace (including people of color, LGBTQ, people with disabilities, and, in many industries, women) tell us that they want to participate in mentoring because they want to increase their exposure and access to more senior people in the organization, and they want to enhance their image in the organization by developing a relationship with someone more senior who can attest to their strengths.

» YOUR TURN «

1. What is your motivation for engaging in mentoring?

_____

_____

_____

_____

2. What do you hope to gain as a mentor or a mentee?

_____

_____

_____

_____

Exploring Differences in How We Learn

Learning is the focus of mentoring. When we train new mentors and mentees, we spend some time helping them discover and understand their learning styles. In training, we often use the 3.1 version of David Kolb's Learning Style Inventory

(LSI).[26] Kolb's LSI focuses on how people perceive and process information, and how we prefer to solve problems, make decisions, manage disagreement, and take in information.[27] While there is some debate in the learning community about the strict validity of learning styles, experiential observations show their practical utility, so it's worth contemplating the questions below.

Kolb's LSI asks you to answer such questions as the following: How do you best take in and process information? Do you need to reflect on information before you take action? Do you learn best by reflecting alone and then sharing your ideas and feelings? Do you perceive information abstractly and then need time to process it and think things through in an organized, rational, data-based manner? Are you more comfortable with a decision that comes from consensus, or do you prefer to reflect on data? Do you perceive information abstractly and process it actively and quickly to find a concrete solution? Do you prefer practice application, or strategic thinking and planning, rather than discussion and consensus building? Do you learn by trial and error? Are you a creative problem solver, risk taker, and change agent? Do you adapt easily to new situations?

We've adapted the chart below (Table 3.2) to help you think about how you learn and interact with others. People demonstrate characteristics in all four quadrants but generally prefer one quadrant or the other. The quadrant that resonates the most may shift depending on the context in which the learning takes place.

For example, Mia has a *converging* learning style. She reaches decisions quickly, sometimes lacking full information. She is viewed by some as making decisions hastily, without taking all factors into account. For people with a converging learning style, the purpose of a meeting is to reach a decision and get things done. Christopher, in contrast, likely has a *diverging* learning style. People with the diverging learning style seek consensus. They like to build relationships before making decisions, and they often see the purpose of meetings as getting people's viewpoints and opinions rather than reaching a decision.

Mia wanted to dive right into goal achievement and was surprised that Christopher wanted to build their relationship first. She found it confusing and even unsettling that he was unwilling to engage right away on her career goals. Christopher felt that Mia was rushing the process and wondered if it was an indication that she valued the outcome over the opportunity to build a relationship. In fact, he was right: for Mia, the time spent on building a relationship seemed like a waste of time.

TABLE 3.2 *Selected learning-style descriptors*

Accommodating	Diverging
Energizing people	Motivating the heart
Visioning	Being imaginative
Motivating	Understanding people
Taking risks	Recognizing problems
Initiating	Brainstorming
Getting things done	Being open-minded
Being adaptable and practical	Valuing harmony

Converging	Assimilating
Exercising personal forcefulness	Using principles and procedures
Solving problems	Planning
Making decisions	Creating models
Reasoning deductively	Defining problems
Valuing efficiency and timeliness	Developing theories
Being practical	Being logical
Setting goals and timelines	Deciding with data

Source: Adapted from Zachary with Fischler, *The Mentee's Guide*, 36.

If more than one learning style seems to resonate with you, ask yourself: When it comes to making decisions, are you more focused on action or reflection? If you focus on action, you are more likely to have a converging learning style or an *accommodating* learning style. If you tend to reflect, you are more likely have a diverging or *assimilating* learning style. In order to feel comfortable with a decision, which of these is more important to you: to know how people feel about the decision, or whether the data support the decision? If you focus more on people, you are more likely to have a diverging or an accommodating learning style. If you value data more when making decisions, you are more likely to have a converging or assimilating learning style.

Once you become aware of your own learning preferences, you can think about the judgments you may be making about people with learning styles different from your own. For example, we often hear from those with diverging learning styles that converging learners come across as too blunt, too quick, and too judgmental. Assimilating learning styles are often perceived by others as too cold or too data-driven, and those with accommodating learning styles as too hasty. Similarly, assimilating learners see diverging learners as spending too much time seeking consensus and checking out others' feelings. Recognizing the judgments we make about others tells us a lot about ourselves. Reflecting in this way helps increase self-awareness about how we take in and process information. In a mentoring relationship, discuss your learning style and that of your mentoring partner's. This helps you both learn more effectively during your mentoring partnership.

We do not live in a world where we operate alone. Culture and identity have a huge impact on us and on how others see us. Creating awareness around identity and culture is critical to the mentoring process, and to understanding what makes up our view of ourselves and what shapes our view of the world. In the next chapter, we'll complete our look at self-awareness preparation with an exploration of bias and privilege in mentoring.

» YOUR TURN «

1. Look at the learning style descriptors chart (Table 3.2). Which learning style do you most seem to prefer?

_____

_____

_____

_____

2. What are some of the judgments you make about people who exhibit other learning styles?

_____

_____

_____

_____

3. Which learning style might challenge the way you prefer to communicate with others?

_____

_____

_____

_____

Chapter Recap

1. Becoming more self-aware is the necessary first step to bridging differences. Without it, you will not be able to identify or understand when you encounter differences that matter.

2. Our culture, background, and identity shape our worldview and how we show up in the world. Only about 20 percent of our identity is visible to others. The 80 percent that lies beneath the surface has a lot to do with how we think of ourselves and act in the world.

3. Once you start to understand what elements of your identity make up your worldview, you'll be better equipped to recognize and understand when and where your mentoring partner's view is different.

4. Keep in mind that two people who come from similar cultures may express their culture differently. Once you have a sense of where you are on various cultural continua, you'll be better able to see how your culture influences how you see the world and how others in your world see you.

5. Learning style can influence how you see others and how others perceive you. Understanding your learning style and your mentoring partner's learning style will help you both learn more effectively during your mentoring partnership.

FOUR

Bias and Privilege in Mentoring

The impact of bias and privilege on how we view ourselves and others cannot be underestimated and is often hard to see—especially when we are looking at ourselves. Yet even though it may be difficult (self-understanding often means going deeper than new mentors and mentees expect or are comfortable with), this is a critical area to explore. As we become aware of own biases and privilege, we also become aware of our assumptions, behavior, and interpretation about the others with whom we interact.

Exploring Bias

Bias is an inclination in favor of or against one thing, person, or group compared with another. It can, and often does, lead to *prejudice*—an adverse judgment or opinion formed without supporting knowledge or facts. It is important to distinguish between the two concepts, since many people whom no one would describe as prejudiced may in fact regularly demonstrate bias. Biases form our own cultural contexts and the conclusions we draw to make sense of observations we have or lessons we learn. Often, they are invisible to those who have them—which is to say, all of us. We may demonstrate bias without being consciously aware that we are doing so.

Although many people don't think they have biases, the fact of the matter is that we are all biased for or against something. Some biases serve us well. For example, as a student, I may develop a bias for languages over science, technology, engineering, and math courses because language arts courses come more easily to me, or because I had a difficult biology class in which I struggled. The bad experience in biology might lead to a prejudice that *all* science classes will be difficult, and I should avoid learning in every related topic. This bias might lead me to discovering and developing my strengths in language or lead me on a path to a career where I use my language skills; or it might disadvantage me, steering me away from courses or subjects that are science based. This could adversely impact me by causing me to avoid classes that challenge me, or it might lead me to a new interest.

In the workplace, bias can be limiting in a way we might not even notice. For example, let's say that I need to hire people who have the skills and competencies lacking on our team. I might have a bias for candidates with certain work experience, training, or prior employers. Perhaps this is because new hires with these qualifications have been successful in the past. My bias may seem to serve me by shortening the length of the hiring process, but by not considering candidates with experience or training with which I am unfamiliar, I might miss out on hiring someone who has a different perspective and outlook that might enhance my team.

In the context of mentoring, bias may prevent us from ever getting to know our partner on anything more than a superficial level—we fail to see the 80 percent below the waterline. For example, my bias may steer me to look for a mentoring partner whom I view as "like me," or to assume that the person I view as "like me" necessarily shares my views. Although this approach seems to serve our mentoring relationship by creating a strong initial connection through our commonality, we both miss out on the benefits of mentoring across differences. Compounding this, if my mentoring partner seems (superficially) to be "like me," I will tend to overlook (and therefore fail to explore) the ways in which we may be different. At best, this results in a missed opportunity for growth and learning; at worst, it leads to a mentoring relationship that has not met its potential.

How Biases Evolve

Biases form from generalizations we make based on our experiences, on how we are raised, on the beliefs we have, and on lessons we learned from friends, family, and others in our environment. Although bias can serve as a shortcut, helping us make quicker decisions, it can also lead to overgeneralization, discrimination, and missed experiences and opportunities.

Sometimes our biases arise from our fears. We create them to help us feel safe, such as a bias against crowds or a bias in favor of a nine-to-five career. As humans, we form biases not just for or against things but also for or against people or groups of people. Many of these biases about people are unconscious and come from cultural conditioning, stereotyping (assumptions about a broad group of people made based on limited data), or generalizing from past experience. We can manage our bias by noticing when we are making decisions or judgments based on fact or based on assumptions that come from generalization or stereotypes.[28]

Managing Our Bias

Learning that we are biased for or against a group of people can be surprising, enlightening, and often disheartening because we envision ourselves as fair and just. The fallacy in this thinking is that if we are biased, we must also be unfair or unjust. We equate being biased with being "bad" in some way. Although bias can lead to prejudice, having bias does not mean we are bad or racist or bigoted. We can manage our bias by being aware of it and working to counteract it by engaging in experiences that lead us to make judgments based on experience rather than on generalization.

Unconscious Bias

The most insidious biases are the ones we are unconscious of. Research shows that most people vastly underestimate the extent to which they are biased.[29] In 1995 three researchers—Tony Greenwald, Mahzarin Banaji, and Brian Nosek—created the Implicit Association Test (IAT), which measures unconscious preference based on a number of categories, including race, age, gender, and sexual orientation.[30] The IAT, a short online assessment offered for free, requires you to associate common adjectives with images to help assess unconscious biases for particular groups and bring these forward so that they can be managed. The results can often be eye-opening (as they were for each of the coauthors).

Unconscious bias shows up in many ways and may not be as straightforward as a preference for a particular race, gender, age, and so on. We may, for example, be biased for or against a certain way of thinking or a specific attitude. This type of bias can take many forms. Taking time to become aware of two types of biases—namely confirmation bias and affinity bias—can help you recognize your own biases when you are exhibiting them.

Confirmation bias: Confirmation bias is the tendency to interpret things in a way that confirms and reinforces your own perceptions or point of view.

After her first meeting with Christopher, Mia was frustrated that they hadn't gotten to goals, but she wasn't surprised. Frankly, it was sort of what she expected. Throughout law school and her legal career, there had been many times her law professors and the partners had talked about the importance of goals, but there were never any concrete suggestions offered and no one ever seemed to make time to talk with her about what she actually wanted to achieve and how she would get there. She had hoped this time might be different, but now it wasn't looking promising.

Notice here how Mia interpreted the meeting to confirm her expectation that the mentoring program was just more unproductive "talk" about goals, instead of merely Christopher's attempt to slow things down and build trust. This is confirmation bias in action: when there are multiple ways to interpret an event or behavior, we find the one that confirms our prior experiences or bias.

Affinity bias: When you gravitate to people with whom you share common interests, traits, or background, you may be demonstrating affinity bias. This is the propensity to prefer people with whom you share an affinity.

Christopher recalled his experience on the advancement committee when the law firm was evaluating associates for partnership. He had voted for Stu, the associate whose career path was most similar to his own. Stu had "grown up" at F3. He had started his career there and dealt with cases like those Christopher had worked on, and he was well-known to the firm leadership. The other candidate, Frank, had come to the law firm just three years before. He had extensive experience in patent litigation, an area with which Christopher was unfamiliar. There was only one spot left for partnership that year. When it came time to vote, Christopher voted for Stu because he was confident that Stu would have acquired the requisite skills needed for partnership along the way.

» YOUR TURN «

1. If you took the IAT earlier, you are probably already thinking about what you've learned about your own biases, and you have probably noticed that there are certain situations in which you are predisposed to a bias or judgment. Jot down your thoughts about that here.

_____

_____

_____

_____

Even if you did not take this test, reflect on your own experiences as you answer the rest of these questions.

2. Where are you looking for evidence to confirm a preconceived judgment or opinion?

_____

_____

_____

3a. Jot down the ten people with whom you most closely associate at work.

_____

_____

_____

3b. Are they similar to you in race, age, gender, sexual orientation, or socioeconomic background? Consider whether you regularly seek the perspective of someone who has a substantially different background from you. How much do you know about the backgrounds of these ten people you've just listed?

_____

_____

_____

_____

4. What can you do to expand the diversity of your inner circle and to create more awareness about their backgrounds and identity?

_____

_____

_____

_____

5. Pay attention to how confirmation bias and affinity bias show up in your daily interactions. What ideas do you have right now to mitigate those biases when you recognize, in real time, that you are demonstrating them?

_____

_____

_____

_____

Exploring Power and Privilege

Privilege is usually tied to socioeconomic status or a specific element of identity (such as level of education or perhaps an Ivy League education) and is often correlated with power, the ability of a group to influence systems and other people.[31] Whereas *bias* is a preference or inclination that results in a conscious or unconscious disadvantage or advantage to others, *privilege* is an unearned *advantage to yourself* that results in a disadvantage to others. What's important to understand is that privilege, like bias, may not be perceived by the person exhibiting it.

In *We Can't Talk about That at Work*, the global organizational development and diversity and inclusion consultant Mary-Frances Winters captures the notion of privilege at its very essence. Privilege, she writes, "refers to the advantages that people benefit from based solely on their social status. It is a status that is conferred by society and perpetuated by systems that favor certain groups. This status is not necessarily asked for or appropriated by individuals, which is why it can be difficult for people to see their own privilege."[32]

The topic of privilege is both misunderstood and sure to ruffle feathers. For those in a dominant group it sometimes feels difficult to swallow that the status they enjoy is, at least in part, due to something that is unearned. After a training at which we (the authors) discussed privilege, a senior white male protested vehemently, "My status is not unearned. I came from nothing and worked hard for what I achieved!" We responded that *recognizing* your privilege was only that— seeing that (in his case) his gender and race automatically privileged him in the mainstream US business culture in which he worked. "It does not mean conceding that your success was easy, that you did not work hard, or that you were handed title, wealth, or anything else," we explained. "It simply gave you a leg up you might not otherwise have had." We could see he was considering it, but it's a hard concept for many people.

Privilege is relative, and dominant groups in society have benefitted the most from unearned power. Whether you have worked hard and been rewarded for your hard work, if you identify with a dominant group (be it race, gender, ethnicity, sexual orientation, or socioeconomic status), you have undoubtedly benefited from some unearned privilege. This doesn't mean you have to feel guilty; but you do need to recognize that others may be experiencing disadvantages you might not be able to begin to understand without meaningful, mutually respectful, and curious dialogue.

It is common for those with privilege not to realize that they have it. One big reason is that we tend to see ourselves as individuals, while others may automatically see us as part of a group. Trying to see ourselves as others see us can be an eye-opening step toward self-awareness and change. In mentoring, the mentor may have an assumed privilege of knowing more about the workplace than the mentee; or the mentor may be in the workplace majority in one or more categories. For example, Mia may automatically view Christopher as a person of privilege because he is a white European male who is a powerful partner in the firm. And she would be correct in her view. For mentors, understanding the privilege that comes with the job is key to understanding their mentoring relationship.

Why does privilege matter so much? If you are interested in the topic of privilege, a must-read early article on the topic is "White Privilege: Unpacking the Invisible Knapsack" by Peggy McIntosh.[33] McIntosh, a white woman, tackles the topic of privilege by race. She lists twenty-six conditions of privilege that white persons can count on, and that African Americans or other people of color do not experience. These include privileges characterized by the following statements:

» If I should need to move, I can be pretty sure of renting or purchasing housing in an area that I can afford and in which I want to live.

» I can be pretty sure that my neighbors in such a location will be neutral or pleasant to me.

» I can go shopping alone most of the time, pretty well assured that I will not be followed or harassed.

» I can turn on the television or open to the front page of the newspaper and see people of my race widely represented.

» Whether I use checks, credit cards, or cash, I can count on my skin color not to work against the appearance of financial reliability.

» I am never asked to speak for all the people of my racial group.

» If my day, week, or year is going badly, I need not ask of each negative episode or situation whether it has racial overtones.

Note that the privilege McIntosh addresses is privilege of skin color, but the same concepts apply to any privilege based on status. "I could think of myself as belonging in major ways," McIntosh notes, "and of making social systems work for me."[34] This concept of presumed belonging is at the heart of privilege, and the key to recognizing privilege is to see where you might have presumed belonging based on some element of your identity (for example, education, sexual orientation, socioeconomic status, gender, native language, ethnicity, etc.) where someone else might not.

Because privilege arises from a presumed sense of belonging, it is important to remember that privilege is not solely the domain of mentors, bosses, or people higher in the org chart. Mentees, too, benefit from privilege, sometimes from privileges their mentors do not have. We often find that, to their detriment, mentoring pairs remember to talk about the privilege of the mentor but forget about the mentee. For example, we've heard the same story from more than one woman in senior management in the technology sector. Often, early in their career, they were the only woman at their organization and struggled to prove themselves in what was (and still is, to a large degree) a man's world. Today, they find themselves successfully mentoring men who automatically benefit from that male privilege. In each case it was eye-opening for the mentee to learn the impact of his privilege on the mentor, and for the mentor to reflect on the personal qualities it takes to face organizational and industry barriers to inclusion.

Finally, what about the person *without* privilege? Just as the person with the privilege may not know they have the privilege, it is quite likely that the person without the privilege *does* recognize that they do not have the same sense of belonging. Not only does this impact opportunity, but it is undoubtedly reflected in their worldview and cultural lens. This, too, is a topic for reflection and discussion between partners.

» YOUR TURN «

1. Look at excerpted statements from McIntosh's list above. How do these resonate with your view of privilege?

   _____

   _____

   _____

   _____

2. Where do you experience a presumed sense of belonging? What does that tell you about the privileges from which you benefit?

   _____

   _____

   _____

   _____

3. Where and when have you experienced a lack of privilege? How might you describe to your mentoring partner the obstacles you have faced as a result?

_____

_____

_____

_____

Now that you have spent some time surfacing your own biases and assumptions, the real differences that lie between you and your mentoring partner begin to become clearer. Next is the "Learn from Differences" part of the book, and we'll begin with preparing the mentoring relationship.

Chapter Recap

1. Everyone is biased. When we take the time for self-awareness, we can explore our biases and manage those biases so that they don't unfairly or unconsciously exclude or disadvantage others.

2. Bias shows up in various ways. Two common kinds of bias are confirmation bias (favoring information that confirms our existing beliefs) and affinity bias (bias toward things/people/beliefs that are "like me").

3. Understanding your privilege (or lack thereof) is important to neutralizing power in a mentoring relationship and relating better to your mentoring partner. Privilege means unearned advantage. If you have privilege, this does not mean that you have not earned what you have, but it does mean that you may have a presumed sense of belonging that others don't have, which makes it more likely that you will succeed in a given situation.

PART II

LEARN *from* DIFFERENCES

Meet Aesha and Heather

At the end of the day, Roger poked his head into Heather's office and asked if she would be open to mentoring Aesha. Aesha started as an intern at Any Healthcare several years ago and has shown tremendous potential for future leadership. Heather didn't need to think twice about it. She was all in!

As she packed up her things before leaving the office, Heather thought back to 1998, when it had been difficult to find her way at Any Healthcare. At first she was excited to be working in health care, where it seemed like changes were afoot everywhere. She yearned to be part of the action, but she didn't feel like much of a contributor. She felt isolated, on the fringes. It had been challenging to adjust to a culture that was neither supportive nor welcoming. She was a single mom and one of only two women in her department.

Heather wanted to be heard and taken seriously. She continued to struggle, as she looked for acceptance and a way to make a meaningful contribution. She hungered to find people whom she could trust. It quickly became clear that she was going to need to become "tough as nails" to succeed. Her struggle to toughen up was a slog, a slow uphill climb. The inside jokes, group speak, and eye-rolling indicated that there was something she was missing. It seemed as if her coworkers all knew something that she wasn't privy to.

Heather was not one to sit by idly. She realized that she had a lot to learn and that she was going to have to own that responsibility. She asked herself, "Who do I know that can help me figure this out?" Then she adopted a divide-and-conquer approach, setting up meetings with each of the department's key players to get to know them and understand the basis of their ideas. It took patience and tenacity, but Heather stuck with it long enough to gain the deeper perspective she needed to understand long-shared history of the department's key players and why things always seemed to go a certain way. Over time, Heather made her mark as a change agent and a high-value contributor.

Aesha was first introduced to Any Healthcare's many product lines while working as an intern at the firm two years earlier. She found the demographics behind consumer marketing fascinating. Following her internship, she was immediately offered a position in the marketing department. Her interest in marketing blossomed, and over time so did her responsibilities.

Aesha started out conducting telephone surveys and before long found herself with increased responsibilities for designing, conducting, and analyzing customer preference surveys. After a year, she discovered her calling and was eager to become a product analyst and team lead for developing and positioning marketing strategies for Any Healthcare's products. She was a quick study and within two years had easily overcome her lack of health-care experience.

Aesha is a first-generation Indian American. Although her husband's parents lived in Mumbai, they visited annually for several months at a time. She looked forward to their visits, but their extended presence added stress to her already long day at work. She didn't see this changing in the short- or long-term and knew that the addition of children in the future would only increase her load. She was trying to figure out how she would manage her time with increasingly competing responsibilities. Aesha loved her work and was excited about upcoming possibilities. Aesha was hoping that her mentor would help her figure out what else she needed to learn, how to establish herself at Any Healthcare, and how to balance work and family.

FIVE

Preparing the Relationship

Making the most of your mentoring relationship requires learning from differences. Once you've prepared yourself by expanding your understanding of your own culture, identity, and biases, you need to get a good sense of who your mentoring partner really is and the differences between you. As the sociologist Milton Bennett has noted, behavior and values must be understood both in terms of the uniqueness of each person and in terms of the culture of that person.[35] There is a bonus! By getting to know your mentoring partner in a deeper way, you may find that you get to know yourself even better. Likely, you will discover that awareness of difference begets more awareness and mutual understanding, which deepens as you explore your differences.

Once Aesha and Heather were settled in with their coffee, Heather launched in. She introduced herself briefly, shared her history at the company, and then described some of the pressures she thought Aesha would face as a young professional with newly acquired health-care experience.

As Aesha listened, one question after another popped up in her head. As Heather kept talking, more questions piled up, and Aesha waited for a break in the story to ask them. Heather, however, continued, offering detailed examples of challenges she had faced in navigating the system, becoming a team member, building successful teams, and hinting at some of the departmental politics that Aesha might face. After ninety minutes, Heather announced that they'd run out of time for the day.

Aesha left Starbucks with her notebook filled with notes and her mind bursting with questions as she tried to process all that she had heard.

Heather didn't know any more about Aesha after their meeting than she did before it. And although Aesha now knew a lot more about Heather, she was curious to learn more and had many unasked questions. This meeting was all about Heather—Aesha, while physically present, was effectively absent. What was going on here? Heather was delighted to be a mentor and eager to share her experience. She knew how difficult it could be to gain a foothold at Any Healthcare, and she'd learned a lot of hard lessons on her way up. Now she wanted to pay it forward by easing Aesha's journey.

Aesha listened, as she felt befitted her role as mentee. Although she had many questions, she didn't want to interrupt Heather or appear disrespectful. Aesha was grateful that Heather had agreed to mentor her but wondered if she would ever be able to really relate. A lot was happening under the surface, but the point here is what *wasn't* going on: a genuine conversation. We've eavesdropped on what Aesha sat through for an hour and a half and seen that without establishing a real connection, mentoring partners can simply go through the motions and never truly engage with each other or with the mentoring process.

Mentoring cannot reach its full potential if you jump right in and don't take time to prepare your relationship adequately. Relationships take work and time to mature. When both parties take the time for self-reflection and to understand each other in a way that goes below the surface, they begin to grow and flourish with good conversation.

The Process: Good Conversation

Good conversation is essential in building and maintaining an effective mentoring relationship. Before we dive more deeply into the process, let's begin with your own experiences.

» YOUR TURN «

Think about a time when you had a really good conversation. What happened that made it a good conversation? What did you and your conversation partner do (the behaviors) and what was going on (the conditions) that made it a good conversation? Make a list of descriptors. (This list can be helpful as a checklist to ensure you stay in good conversation.)

_____

_____

_____

_____

The Five Levels of Conversation

Mentoring conversations are built on a foundation of trust. Learning increases as the conversation moves from basic information transaction to a genuine collaboration and dialogue. Our levels of conversation model (Figure 5.1) illustrates the five levels of conversation and their relationship to building trust and promoting learning in a mentoring relationship.[36]

1. **Monologue:** The levels begin with monologue, where one person grabs most of the airspace and ends up doing all the talking. Sometimes mentors in particular get trapped in monologue. Out of nerves, a desire to teach, or a lack of awareness, they launch into their stories and become the "sage on the stage," attempting to impart knowledge rather than create dialogue. This is what happened with Aesha and Heather in their first meeting. Heather relayed her own journey and lessons to Aesha without allowing any time for Aesha to respond or ask questions.

2. **Transaction:** In the next level, transaction, an exchange of questions and answers occurs in which talk remains on the surface. Most conversations are merely transactions. A transactional mentoring conversation can feel like a checklist or a recitation of a set of to-dos. It might sound like this:

MENTOR: "Did you read the article I sent you?"

MENTEE: "Yes, I did, thanks."

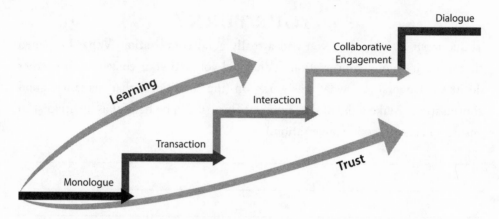

FIGURE 5.1   Levels of Conversation Model

Source: © 2019, Center for Mentoring Excellence. The figure was developed by the Center for Mentoring Excellence and is described in Zachary and Fischler, *Starting Strong*, 166.

MENTOR: "Have you had you had an opportunity to talk with my sponsor?"

MENTEE: "I am happy to report it happened last week."

The back-and-forth exchange might seem like an efficient way to report progress or hold a mentee accountable for the progress, but the exchange is inherently limiting. It doesn't generate much energy and satisfaction and does not result in real learning for either party.

3. Interaction: The third level, interaction, gets closer to good conversation, but it is not quite there yet. It often focuses on "how to" and "where to" rather than "why." Interactions promote knowledge transfer but limit opportunities for insights, reflection, or discovery. For example, a mentee shares her current work struggle, and her mentor tries to make her feel better by stating, "I've felt that way myself many times. I wouldn't worry about it." The mentee might learn more if her mentor were instead to have asked her *why* she thinks the problem is occurring, or what's going on that makes her think there is a problem. The mentor may learn more from that answer as well. Often, conversations where mentoring partners get to know each other fall into this category. Mentoring partners exchange personal information and career stories. Certainly this is both a useful and important conversation, where comfort and trust begin to build. However, for mentoring to be effective, conversations must eventually move beyond interaction.

4. Collaborative engagement: The fourth level, collaborative engagement, is where deeper insight and reflection take place. Once trust has been established, mentoring partners are willing to be vulnerable. As trust deepens, the relationship becomes stronger. The mentor learns something new about the mentee, and the mentee begins to understand that the mentor is a person who also struggled and learned along her own career path.

Aesha and Heather, for example, are still in monologue. It will likely take them a while to move through transaction and on to collaborative engagement, but it is important that they do. In the collaborative engagement stage, curiosity can move mentoring pairs forward in a significant way because there is a mutuality of need-to-know that propels conversation and compels mentoring partners to learn more and be more open to understanding differing perspectives. With increased collaborative engagement, learning can accelerate and take the partnership to a whole new level.

5. Dialogue: Dialogue, the fifth level of conversation, leads to transformational thinking that generates shared understanding from the mutual learning that is taking place. Once trust is high, there can be an open exchange of ideas without defensiveness. Sudden insights grow into new understandings. On this level, there is no debate, and no attempt to convince or change the other person's mind about something. Both parties expand their understanding as they learn, explore, and grow. There is excitement about their learning and that expands in tandem with the new understandings they create.

Building Trust: Creating Conversations that Dig Deeper

As the days wore on, Heather's stories and experiences sparked even more questions for Aesha. Although she admired Heather and hoped to be as successful, she seriously wondered if Heather had a life outside of work. Aesha sure hoped so, because she was not interested in a career that left no time for home and family. She had been expecting to get some guidance from her mentor on how to balance home and work life. She had thought that Heather might have some insight about this because she had been a single mom when she started at Any Healthcare, but it hadn't come up. Aesha made herself a reminder to talk with Heather about it later but then decided instead to text Heather and ask her about it. Here's how that exchange went:

Aesha: "Good meeting! You have a ton to offer. After we cover all the things you want to cover, I'd like to get your views on work-life balance on the agenda. Can we talk about that next time?"

When Heather received Aesha's text, her initial response was to chuckle. She'd given up the hope of achieving any sort of balance long ago. She'd realized early on in her career that if she wanted to be successful it had to be career first. The only way she had known to provide for her son, Matthew, was to have a well-paying career so he could have some stability. Thankfully, Heather's mother and some great care providers had been there to help with her son. Achievement at work had never been a question for Heather: she had always felt compelled to say yes to all opportunities and to be the hardest working executive. The rest would work itself out. She took a breath and texted Aesha.

Heather: "I enjoyed our meeting too. Is there really such a thing as work-life balance??? 😉 "

Aesha was confused. She felt dismissed. Was Heather signaling that she was not interested in talking about how Aesha could manage her work obligations and still have time for family? Aesha concluded that it was best not to bring up these concerns about work-life balance again and omitted the topic from the agenda she was preparing for their next meeting. Instead, she decided to find out what Heather's expectations were for the mentoring relationship and added that to the agenda.

From the beginning, Heather assumed that Aesha was like her and wanted to get ahead, and that therefore Aesha wanted and needed the same things that Heather did when she started at Any Healthcare. Heather assumed that because Aesha was a woman, their wants, needs, and career paths would be similar. When those assumptions turned out to be erroneous, Heather simply made new assumptions. For example, when Aesha persisted in wanting to talk about family, Heather immediately assumed that Aesha wasn't as serious about her professional success as she was.

Heather began to notice her own irritation every time Aesha brought up feeling guilty or torn between family and work, thinking, "Aesha just doesn't have what it takes to succeed." When Heather realized that she was making that conclusion, she felt guilty and a bit conflicted. On the one hand, Heather was proud of her own commitment to work and firmly believed that success in the industry required a 100 percent commitment. On the other hand, as she had gotten to know Aesha, she knew that her mentee had the smarts to succeed, and she'd begun learning about how real the pull of home life was for Aesha. Heather was growing concerned that her own inability to relate was preventing her from mentoring Aesha effectively.

All at once, Heather became acutely aware of her own bias for compartmentalizing work from home life and that she was making judgments about Aesha and other colleagues who wanted more balance. She started to notice her bias in action. When a colleague wasn't fully committed to work, for example, Heather would look for other evidence to support this conclusion—maybe it was that they took an extra lunch break, or were sick one day, or that they took a bit too long to finish an assignment. Heather really did not want to do this with Aesha, so she made a special effort to look for supporting evidence that the colleagues she had previously judged negatively actually were committed to their work. She was surprised that once she started looking, she found more positive clues quite easily.

Heather was kicking herself now. Why had she treated Aesha's text about work-life balance so lightly? She could see, in retrospect, how she had shut Aesha down without a second thought. There could have been so much more learning for both Aesha and Heather if Heather had acknowledged Aesha's need to discuss this topic and gotten curious about why the demands of family life might have been such a pressing concern for Aesha.

Assumptions

Everyone holds assumptions about how the world works, and we view life through these filters. We take action based on our assumptions, and therefore they become "our truth." But (and this is an essential point to recognize) they are not necessarily *the* truth in any given situation. In the mentoring relationship, our assumptions about what is true, what is appropriate, and how people should behave can prevent us from seeing what is true about ourselves, our mentoring partners, and the environments in which we work.

In the following example, notice how assumption affects perception. When she was practicing law, coauthor Lisa sometimes represented clients seeking asylum in the United States. In order to have a successful claim, asylum seekers must demonstrate that they have a credible fear of persecution if they were to return home. If the fear could be deemed reasonable by a judge, the client's claim might succeed. If not, it would likely fail. When she met these clients for the first time, Lisa's first task was to assess whether they were telling the truth about their fear of returning home.

Lisa was raised in the United States and shared a common cultural assumption that people who are telling the truth look you in the eye and people who are lying will avert their eyes. When she first met Katherine, a client from Uganda, Katherine did not look her in the eye. Automatically, Lisa concluded that Katherine was not being truthful. She judged everything she heard from that point forward through the lens that Katherine did not have a credible claim. Fortunately, Katherine was naturally skilled in cultural competency. Not too far into the conversation, she paused and said, "I want you to know why I am looking down. Americans make eye contact out of respect. In my culture, when you are in the presence of someone you respect, you do not meet their gaze. It is therefore difficult for me to look you in the eye." Katherine's astuteness was a check on Lisa's assumptions. Once this difference was called out, Lisa was able to listen to Katherine's story with an open mind and represent her in her successful claim for asylum.

All of us, inevitably, have assumptions about others and about our roles that guide our behavior and contribute to us forming conscious and unconscious bias. The key to understanding our assumptions is to bring them to the surface so we can test them for validity and challenge them if necessary. Adult educator Stephen Brookfield talks about the process of "assumption hunting."[37] He breaks it down into three interrelated phases: (1) identifying assumptions, (2) checking them for accuracy, and (3) acting in a more inclusive and integrative way.

Assumption hunting is especially important in a mentoring context. No mentoring partner is well served if they are in a mentoring relationship that is based on misunderstanding. Relying on invalid assumptions can undermine mentoring relationships by making them vulnerable to missteps and misinterpretation. Assumptions are woven deeply into what we consider normal behavior, so assumption hunting can be challenging. Yet, actively seeking to identify them is essential because it helps us realize the judgments we unconsciously make when reality differs from our assumptions. Aesha assumed that her mentor would understand her concerns since they were both working women. Heather assumed that if Aesha wanted to succeed, her mentee would need to make the same career choices that she had.

Testing out assumptions with your mentoring partner—about each other and about your roles as mentor and mentee—is essential. In the long run it will help you manage and meet each other's expectations and avoid missteps. Untested assumptions can undermine trust and communication, and they can perpetuate bias, judgment, and misunderstanding. Assumption hunting helps raise awareness about why we do things. We'll talk more about this in the next chapter.

» YOUR TURN «

1. If someone were to view the visible part of your iceberg, what assumptions might they make about you?

   _____

   _____

   _____

   _____

2. What assumptions do you have about the role of a mentor and the role of a mentee?

   _____

   _____

   _____

   _____

3. What assumptions do you have about the way your mentoring partner should approach the mentoring relationship?

   _____

   _____

   _____

   _____

Table 5.1 lists some assumptions that mentors and mentees often mention in our workshops. Do any of these resonate with you?

Curiosity

Once you have uncovered some of your assumptions about your mentoring partner, the next step is to test those assumptions for accuracy. To do this, you must use some constructive curiosity. This is not being nosy. Genuine curiosity springs from your authentic desire to understand something more deeply. Earlier in this book

TABLE 5.1 *Common assumptions about mentoring*

Assumptions about the role of mentee	Assumptions about the role of mentor	Assumptions about mentoring
» The mentee knows what they want from mentoring.	» The mentor has the answers.	» Mentoring doesn't require much preparation.
» The mentee has clear goals.	» The mentor wants the mentee to succeed.	» I've been in a mentoring relationship before, so I know how to do it.
» The mentee is looking for answers from the mentor.	» The mentor will be available whenever the mentee needs them.	» I know how to manage people, so I will be a good mentor.
» The mentee has to follow the mentor's advice.	» The mentor understands the mentee and the mentee's motivation.	» Mentoring is the key to promotion.
» The mentee aspires to be like the mentor.	» The mentor has mentored before and understands what is needed to be a good mentor.	» Mentoring is organic and just develops over time.
» The mentee wants to rise in the organization.		
» The mentee will dedicate the time necessary to make the most of mentoring.		

Source: Authors.

we cited a *Harvard Business Review* article that defined curiosity as "a penchant for seeking new experiences, knowledge, and feedback and an openness to change."[38]

The authors of that article found that curiosity is the best predictor of leadership competency and that, if appropriate developmental opportunities are offered, curious leaders are usually able to advance to C-level roles.[39] A mentoring relationship can be an excellent laboratory to cultivate curiosity and find the right developmental opportunities. "Curiosity," say these authors, "reduces our susceptibility to stereotypes and to confirmation bias."[40] We have found that curiosity boosts business performance as well as mentor and mentee performance. It inspires mentor and mentees to develop more trusting and more collaborative relationships with one another.

Behavioral scientist Francesca Gino found that "when our curiosity is triggered, we are less likely to fall prey to confirmation bias and to stereotyping people."[41] Curiosity encourages members of a group to put themselves in one another's shoes and take an interest in one another's ideas rather than focus only on their own perspective.[42] Mentoring partners can encourage curiosity simply by being inquisitive. When a mentor or mentee asks questions instead of presuming to know answers, they are practicing what Gino calls "intellectual humility"—the ability to acknowledge that what they know is limited. This, of course, requires a growth mindset (discussed in Chapter 2). Curiosity is especially important when faced with situations, attitudes, or behaviors we don't understand. By *exercising curiosity* (that is, proactively practicing it), we seek to get more information before we reach conclusions, minimizing the extent to which we judge our mentoring partners and allowing us to suspend judgment so that we can better understand and appreciate differences.

As Heather would have discovered if she had taken the time to get to know Aesha more deeply, Aesha deeply values family. In Aesha's cultural framework, as a daughter-in-law she is expected to care for her husband's visiting parents during what many Americans might view as a very lengthy stay. Aesha understands this, accepts her role, and is happy to host her in-laws; but she does wonder how she is going to get everything done that she needs to do. Fortunately, though Heather was initially dismissive of Aesha's concerns about meeting family obligations, Heather eventually got curious about the pull that family obligations had on Aesha.

As Heather gradually understood that Aesha's concerns were deep and real, the dynamic between them started to shift for the better. Heather, who had been judgmental and mildly annoyed about Aesha's early insistence that they address "balance," began to see the influence of Aesha's culture on her sense of familial obligation. Heather suddenly understood that Aesha couldn't be comfortable making the same choice Heather had when weighing work and family obligations. More important, Heather started to question whether that would even be essential for Aesha's success. Aesha gave a deep sigh of relief as she saw that Heather was beginning to understand Aesha as an individual rather than a Heather clone.

Creating space within your mentoring relationship to ask questions and explore answers helps cultivate curiosity and accelerate getting to know one another better. Many mentoring pairs we coach set aside time at the beginning of each meeting to ask each other "power questions" that will help them understand what makes the other tick. Some questions they have come up with include: "What is an ideal day?" "What is your superpower?" and "What motivates you?" While general catch-ups can be helpful in mentoring conversations toward building trust, questions like these go a bit deeper and allow mentoring partners to connect in a way that encourages further questions and dispels judgment.

» YOUR TURN «

1. Think of a time when you felt curious about someone. How did you demonstrate your curiosity? What prompted your curiosity?

_____

_____

_____

_____

2. With your mentoring partner, brainstorm a list of power questions to use to get to know each other better and cultivate an environment of curiosity. Set aside five minutes at the beginning of each meeting for each of you to answer one power question.[43]

_____

_____

_____

_____

3. Practice curiosity. Find one opportunity each day to reframe a statement into a question and really listen for the answer. What do you notice?

_____

_____

_____

_____

Asking Questions

Good questions are critical in expressing curiosity, generating conversation, creating developmental relationships, building networks, and developing trust. James E. Ryan, dean of the Harvard School of Business, suggests six questions that are "everyday staples of simple and profound conversation."[44] We focus here on four of those questions that are particularly germane to mentoring.[45]

Wait, What?

Ryan's first question is—"Wait, what?"— and it's easy to understand why. "Wait" signifies a pause. "What" begs clarification. Asking "Wait, what?" is an effective way of clarifying thinking and it invites others to do the same.[46] It reminds us to slow down and wait, to make sure we truly understand what's being said before we act/react. According to Ryan, "Wait, what?" is a clarifying question that is at the root of all understanding.[47]

I Wonder If...?

The second question—"I wonder if...?" or "I wonder why...?"—lies at the heart of all curiosity. It is useful for both mentoring partners because it invites a level of engagement that deepens the conversation. It is how we prompt ourselves and others to try something new, and how we deepen our understanding of one another's motivations and perspectives.

These questions are particularly important when our mentoring partners' approach or mindset is different than our own. Summoning a sense of wonder can heighten our awareness and help us come up with more innovative, tailored, and sticky solutions. Aesha wondered why Heather kept dismissing her request to talk about balance. She sensed it was a taboo topic, but it wasn't until she asked "why?" that she started to understand Heather better.

Couldn't We at Least...?

The third question—"Couldn't we at least...?"—is another power question. It's a great way to get unstuck because merely asking it helps create common ground and triggers other questions. Best of all, it keeps people in conversation. Ryan sees this question as the "heart of all progress"; by sparking momentum it keeps us moving forward. "It is the question," he says, that "recognizes that journeys are often long and uncertain, that problems will not be solved with one conversation and that even the best efforts will not always work."[48]

How Can I Help?

The fourth question—"How can I help?"—is the foundation of all good relationships. "How you help matters just as much as that you do help," Ryan explains, "which is why it is essential to begin by asking How can I help? If you start with this question you are asking with humility for direction. You are recognizing that others are experts in their own lives, and you are affording them the opportunity to remain in charge, even if you are providing some help."[49]

Mentors, this is a great question, and you may be tempted to start your very first mentoring session by asking it. Beware that your mentee may not yet know what they need, nor have you built enough trust for them to feel comfortable answering you honestly so early in the relationship.

How to Ask Good Questions

Good questions are expansive. They unlock possibilities, set the stage for deeper conversations, and build trust. Ryan's questions are a good start, but curious people should ask many more questions. Sometimes the most generative response to a mentoring partners' statement is a question that seeks to go deeper. Such questions can elicit more facts, or seek to create a deeper understanding of mindset, feelings, and rationale. We'll explore some of these types of questions below.

Probing questions usually start with what journalists call the 5W1H: What? Where? Who? When? Why? and How? These open-ended questions are designed for fact-gathering—they cannot be answered with a simple yes or no. (Will? or Did? questions are closed because they solicit a yes or no answer that effectively ends the conversation.) Effective probing questions create shared understanding of what actually occurred.

For example, Heather might ask her mentee: Who might you need to involve in helping you with the design of your presentation? What happened when you pitched your deck to the senior leadership team? When or where did the pitch take place? Why did you feel uncomfortable sharing the deck with your supervisor in advance? How will you follow up? Aesha might ask Heather: Who were your mentors? What support did they provide that made a difference in your career? When did you feel like you had gained enough experience to lead a team? Where did you feel you made the biggest difference in the company? How did you build your network?

Since conversation is not interrogation, both mentor and mentee can use probing questions to illuminate issues. Once you have gathered sufficient information through probing questions, you might use *clarifying questions* to create mutual understanding about the facts. Clarifying questions are also open-ended. They are designed to help us understand motivation, behavior, and context around the facts. These questions acknowledge the information received from the probing questions and dig deeper. The best clarifying questions begin with a statement that paraphrases the information received and then uses that information as the basis of the next question. For example:

» "It sounds to me like you are saying that you are getting mixed signals from your manager about what she wants you to do next." (Paraphrasing) "Is that correct?" (Clarifying)

» "You feel really conflicted about pursuing this project." (Paraphrasing) "What does that mean for you?" (Clarifying)

» "I can tell you need some clarity around this." (Paraphrasing) "How do you define that?" (Clarifying)

Clarifying questions can also be quite useful when you don't understand or when you disagree with your mentoring partner. Be sure your question seeks clarification but does not appear judgmental. For example: "I hear that you are concerned that your manager isn't pleased with you." (Paraphrasing) "What about her reaction makes you think that?" (Clarifying)

Avoid at all costs the judgmental version of these interactions: "I hear you are concerned your manager isn't pleased with you. I think you're reading it wrong." Or, "I understand you feel concerned, but I don't think you should feel that way." We are so used to making judgments that it becomes automatic to offer our opinions. It can be difficult to switch from a position of judgment to clarification, yet doing so is vitally important to your relationship. A question asked with judgment will result in (a) either a nonresponse or (b) a defensive answer or (c) an answer that is crafted to appease your judgment. In any of those cases, judgment contracts and hampers trust. Making the switch takes awareness and practice, but it's a critical skill for both mentors and mentees to learn and use.

Listening

As thought leader Stephen Covey said, "Seek first to understand and then to be understood."[50] This is the key to listening, and listening is the key to asking good questions. Good listening demands our full attention. It requires paying attention to the other person's words, intonation, and body language from start to finish. When you are listening well, you are not already planning what you are going to say in response while another person is speaking. Rather, you are listening all the way until the end and responding to what you actually heard.

Significantly, good listening also requires that you pay attention to cultural context. You will need to be aware of your mentoring partner's preference for direct or indirect communication. Individuals with a preference for direct communication tend to prefer precise and explicit language, put value on speaking their mind, and prefer to verbally assert their difference in opinion. The meaning in their conversations is conveyed primarily through words.[51] For individuals with a preference for indirect communication, the meaning comes from the surrounding context, and the speaker often leaves it to the listener to pick up the clues. Both styles can be effective, but it is critical to good listening that you know your own preference and recognize (without judgment) the style of your mentoring partner.

Coauthor Lisa's cultural preference is direct communication, which was commonplace when she lived in Chicago. But when she moved to her company's Pacific Northwest location, she encountered a stark cultural divide. There, the general organizational culture was more indirect. In her first few weeks at the new location, Lisa presented a strategic plan on a diversity initiative to a meeting full of stakeholders, hoping to seek alignment so she could roll out the plan. When she was done presenting, the room was quiet but the attendees all nodded their heads. Lisa asked if there were questions or concerns, but there were none. Several attendees gave her a thumbs-up. She left the meeting feeling like she had agreement.

Once Lisa started to implement the initiative, however, one of the stakeholders approached her to say they were not in fact aligned with the initiative. Lisa felt blindsided and confused. After all, there had been head nods and thumbs-up but no objections or questions. Lisa learned quickly (and the hard way!) that in this culture head nods and thumbs-up can mean "I hear you" and "I understand," not necessarily "I agree" or "I am aligned." The silence and lack of questions were meant to be indirect signals of lack of agreement, not assent. Now Lisa uses this awareness to "listen" to the silence and more explicitly state her understanding.

Have you ever been in a conversation where the other person said something that you couldn't understand, but you nodded as if you understood so that you didn't have to ask for clarification? This happens to many of us, and the intent is often well-meaning (for example, to avoid embarrassing the other person, because you have a hearing impairment, to save time, to not be "rude" by asking the other person to repeat). However—particularly when the native language of mentoring partners differs, or when one member of a mentoring partnership has an accent or speech impediment, and particularly when someone is sharing something personal—ask them to repeat what they said. The conversations in mentoring are deep and important. Pretending to understand can later result in the person feeling dismissed, ignored, or misunderstood. Take the time to ask for clarification.

Here are a few other rules of good listening:

» Good listening requires you to minimize distractions. Obvious distractions are email and phones. Often people will have their phones out but turned over on the table in front of them. Research has shown that the mere presence of a cell phone or smartphone can lessen the quality of conversation, reducing the amount of empathy exchanged.[52] Best practice? Put your phone out-of-sight.

» Good listening requires that you listen all the way to the end before you comment. Do you often find yourself nodding while formulating your response to something someone is saying? When you do this, you miss the full context of what is being said. Instead, wait until the end and take advantage of a good long pause to determine how you wish to respond.

» Good listening requires that you listen to understand, not to wait for an opening. Good conversations are not a game of ping-pong, where participants alternate speaking one after another. To be responsive requires you to be fully in the conversation, and not waiting for your chance to get a word in.

» Good listening requires paying attention to tone, body language, and facial expression, not just to the words used (Table 5.2). In a well-cited study, psychologist Albert Mehrabian found that when people talk about their feelings or attitudes, the meaning of a message is conveyed significantly more by tone of voice and body language than by the words used by the speaker.[53]

TABLE 5.2 *Body language matters*

What we do	Level of influence
Our words	7%
Tone of voice	38%
Body language	55%

Source: Mehrabian, *Silent Messages*.

» YOUR TURN «

1. If you were to give yourself a grade as a listener, what would it be and why?

_____

_____

_____

_____

2. What are your strengths as a listener?

_____

_____

_____

_____

3. What are three specific actions you can take to strengthen your listening skills over the next ninety days?

_____

_____

_____

_____

Preparing the mentoring relationship requires mentoring partners to learn about one another, seek clarification, and build trust. This happens only by cultivating curiosity, asking questions, and deep listening. In the next chapter, we'll explore the fine art of simply getting to know one another.

Chapter Recap

1. Sometimes we think we are having a conversation, but we are really engaged in a monologue or a transaction. Mentoring conversations should strive for higher levels of conversation: collaborative engagement or dialogue. The higher the level of conversation, the more it promotes learning and deepens trust.

2. Since we act on our assumptions, we need to test them out and see if they are valid before we come to a conclusion. This is particularly important when it comes to cultural context. Listening for context requires curiosity. Curiosity requires intellectual humility and a growth mindset.

3. There are many types of questions we can ask to generate conversation and develop trust. Mentors and mentees should practice the art of asking the good questions.

4. Good listening requires that you minimize distractions, listen all the way to the end, listen to understand, and pay attention to tone, body language, and facial expression.

SIX

Getting to Know Each Other

Simply getting to know one another should be the focus of all or most of your first few interactions of the mentoring relationship. Sometimes these interactions happen live, in the initial mentoring meetings. Some mentors and mentees like to interact by email in advance of the first meeting. Like every other step along the way, getting to know each other requires reflection, planning, and (where possible) outreach to your mentoring partner.

Take Time to Build Trust by Getting to Know Each Other

Getting to know each other is not something you can check off your list in one conversation. Rather, it develops over a series of conversations early in your mentoring relationship. Let's return to Mia and Christopher from Part 1 and step back a bit in time to find out how they first got to know each other.

Mia stepped into Christopher's office and proffered an enthusiastic handshake. She told him that she was eager to learn about his career path. How had he achieved his stature and reputation? What would she need to do to follow in his footsteps as a go-to labor and employment attorney? She explained why and what she wanted to learn from him and expressed gratitude that he had agreed to mentor her.

Christopher could see that Mia was committed to her professional growth. Clearly, she had come prepared for their first mentoring meeting. A good sign. But she spoke so quickly, hurrying from one topic to the next, that he was thrown off his game. In response, he moderated the speed of his own speech, hoping that it would slow her down. When it didn't, he realized he might have to address this issue, but it would have to come later in their relationship. Maybe she was nervous. Or maybe it was just a generational thing. He decided to ignore it for now.

When Mia finally took a breath, Christopher jumped in. "You have lots of questions, Mia, but I'd like to get to know you a bit before we get into all that. Tell me about why you became an attorney. And why did you choose labor and employment?"

Even though their early relationship was marred by miscommunications, Christopher was 100 percent correct to slow Mia's self-introduction and try to understand her motivations for mentoring. In our work we long ago lost count of the number of times mentoring pairs have come to us wondering why they haven't made consistent progress, only to discover that they skipped over the getting-to-know-you phase of the mentoring relationship and headed right to goal setting.

Like Mia, many of us have a bias for action, and we all want to feel as if we are making the most of our time together. We understand how tempting it is for people to skip right into what they think is the heart of the mentoring relationship: goal setting and goal achievement. Mentees want to feel like they are making the most of their mentors' time. Mentors want to feel like they are adding value. Both mentor and mentee often feel like the trust will build organically over time. Yet as our mentoring model shows (see Figure 1.1), and as our discussion of the levels of conversation further illustrates (see Figure 5.1), preparing the relationship is an essential first step in building trust—a necessary part of meaningful mentoring conversation.

So how do you do it? This is where the time spent on self-reflection proves its worth. If you know who your prospective mentoring partner is ahead of time, exchange introductory emails before your first meeting. This allows you to set the tone for your mentoring relationship. We encourage you to be a bit vulnerable and model the free exchange of information that you hope will occur once you meet. Share something you have learned about yourself, your motivation for engaging in a mentoring relationship, and ask a few questions that prompt your mentoring partner's reflection and help them best prepare for your meeting together. Allow enough time before the first meeting to send, receive, reflect upon, and reply to each other's emails.

Making the connection—which is the essence of getting to know one another and building trust—is the most critical element in laying a strong foundation for a mentoring partnership. Even if you don't know who your prospective mentoring partner is ahead of time, you can still reflect on what you want to share. This is an opportune time to revisit the identity iceberg discussed in Chapter 3. Think of a few elements of your personal iceberg that impact the way you are viewed and the way you view the world that you can share with your mentoring partner.

» YOUR TURN «

1. What three things about your identity will you share with your mentoring partner in an introductory email or in your first meeting?

_____

_____

_____

_____

2. What is your motivation for mentoring? Prepare yourself to share why you are committed to mentoring.

_____

_____

_____

_____

3. What are three things that you want to ask your mentoring partner in an introductory email or in your first mentoring meeting? Note that these should be questions that you are prepared to answer for yourself as well.

_____

_____

_____

_____

Share Some of Your Own Guiding Principles

In our workshops we often ask participants to share a piece of wisdom they treasure that might help their mentoring partner understand what is meaningful to them personally or professionally. Whenever we do this exercise, it yields some rich quotes or truisms, and these help us learn a lot about their mindset and philosophies. We encourage participants to share these with their mentoring partners. Here are some examples:

» "The main thing is to keep the main thing the main thing."

» "People will forget what you did. People will forget what you said. But people will never forget how you made them feel." (Maya Angelou)

» "The most important thing is to show up."

» "Don't shoot the arrow until you are certain your target is in sight."

» "Make the time to take the time."

» "Be so good that people can't ignore you."

Learning about your mentoring partner's guiding principles can help set the stage for learning and may even help you learn more about yourself. Often, words of wisdom like these can help uncover cultural reference points that reveal very different ways of thinking about a particular topic. Here are some examples of different beliefs around certain concepts that reflect different viewpoints.

» "The squeaky wheel gets the grease" versus "Don't speak unless it improves upon silence."

» "Good better best, never let it rest until your good is better and your better is best" versus "Don't let the perfect be the enemy of the good."

» "The first to raise their voice loses the argument" versus "Silence produces peace and peace produces safety."

Take the time to consider how your words of wisdom reflect and are influenced by your own culture.

» YOUR TURN «

1. Identify some guiding principles/concepts that you treasure and try to live by.

_____

_____

_____

_____

2. Pick one principle/concept that relates to mentoring and that you would be willing to share with your mentoring partner.

_____

_____

_____

_____

3. What are some examples of how you honor that guiding principle or concept on a regular basis?

_____

_____

_____

_____

Share Your Career Highlights and Milestones

It may seem an obvious step but the utility of learning more about your mentoring partner's career and work experience before your first mentoring meeting is worth stressing. For mentees, it can help provide context and open up potential connection points or questions they can ask their mentor. For mentors, it can provide context and points of connection with your mentee. To this end, it can be helpful to obtain a copy of your mentoring partner's bio or CV in advance of the first mentoring meeting. One note of caution, however: do not use a mentoring partner's

CV solely as a vehicle for finding commonality. Remember that there is value in uncovering and inquiring about difference. The best way to use this information is to stoke your curiosity about each experience rather than to prejudge or simply look for the things you have in common.

Many years ago, coauthor Lois led a team of six evaluators that assessed student levels of intellectual and ethical development. To guide them in their assessments, they relied on a set of specific qualitative criteria. After each evaluator independently assigned numerical ratings, the team met to reach consensus on their ratings. While using a majority decision might have been easier and more expedient, the team needed to agree on the final ratings and that meant accommodating different points of view (not easy to do with six independent evaluators). There were often differences in their individual assessments. Each member of the team tenaciously held onto their own point of view and tried to convince the others they had the right answer. Lois realized that if team members didn't get curious about where each of them was coming from, they were never going to make progress.

This proved hard to accomplish and took discipline. As the team's conversations continued, relationships among the group members strengthened and everyone's understanding expanded. Through this experience, Lois learned the value of asking questions to stimulate dialogue and get differences out on the table, a skill she continues to use in presentations, workshops, and group facilitations to this day. Lois's mentees repeatedly tell her how much they appreciate the thoughtful questions she asked that led them on their own journeys of self-awareness and discovery. She tells her mentees this story to let them know in advance that she will be asking tough questions throughout the process. She also tells them why she thinks this is necessary.

» YOUR TURN «

1. Take the time to reflect on your career journey so that you can eventually share these with your mentoring partner. What opportunities helped you grow and develop?

_____

_____

_____

_____

2. What did you learn about yourself as a result of each opportunity?

_____

_____

_____

_____

3. What lessons will you share with your mentoring partner?

_____

_____

_____

_____

Share Mentoring Stories

When Aesha learned that she was going to be a part of the mentoring program, she was excited, but a bit dubious about whether it would make a difference. The last mentor she had was when she was in graduate school. When she entered her master's program in business analytics, she had been assigned Debbie, a PhD student, as her mentor. It seemed like Debbie's role was to make sure that Aesha was equipped to get a job at management consulting, something Debbie and many other students aspired to. After the first two meetings (in which Debbie had provided Aesha with a checklist of qualities she needed to work on and had given her what seemed to Aesha to be meaningless assignments) the relationship had fizzled and Aesha remembered feeling more alone than ever.

She was glad that she would now have Heather to guide her at Any Healthcare, but she wanted to make sure that mentoring this time would be different than her experience with Debbie. Would it sound like she was complaining if she shared this story with Heather?

Aesha decided to tell Heather about her mentoring experience with Debbie and mustered the courage to share it at their third meeting. Heather listened, then told Aesha that she herself had not participated in a formal mentoring program before. "All of my experiences with mentors have been informal." Heather acknowledged, "I always just found someone I could identify with who was doing what I wanted to do and tried to be like them."

Heather heard herself say this and inwardly cringed. She realized that she had never consciously thought about the kind of leader she wanted to be. There hadn't been many women in positions of influence when she had started, so she tried to emulate the men at the top. In many instances it worked, and she was given increasingly more complex work assignments and many promotions. But Heather never really felt close to anyone on the team and didn't share much about herself with her colleagues. She wondered if that would ever change for her, but she didn't share her thoughts with Aesha. Instead, Heather said, "I'm eager to try something more structured with you now. Maybe we will both learn something."

Sharing stories about your mentoring experiences serves several purposes. First, it helps mentoring partners get to know each other better. Second, by reflecting on what worked and what didn't, and on the other person's depth of experience with mentoring, each person can get clues about how the other learns and how the mentee might be best supported and challenged. Finally, it provides helpful information when setting agreements about the mentoring relationship. (We'll discuss setting agreements in the next chapter.)

» YOUR TURN «

1. What is your experience with mentoring?

_____

_____

_____

_____

2. What worked and what didn't?

_____

_____

_____

_____

3. When you look back on prior mentoring experiences, what do you want to carry forward to your current relationship?

_____

_____

_____

_____

Share Your Assumptions about Mentoring

As you learned in Chapter 5, unchecked assumptions about mentoring can lead to misunderstanding and miscommunication. If you feel the need for more clarity, ask for it. For example, Heather had assumed that her role as mentor was to impart wisdom. Accordingly, she relayed to Aesha the lessons she had learned from a difficult time in her career so that her mentee could avoid the struggles that Heather had faced. Aesha, for her part, had assumed that it was her role as a mentee to bring her own questions about learning, establishing credibility, and managing competing demands of work and family. Neither of these perspectives are wrong, and they may not even be incompatible. However, if they fail to discuss this early in the relationship, both Aesha and Heather may be left feeling disappointed in how they accomplished their own role, or on how their mentoring partner lived up to her role. Worse yet, they may feel like mentoring has not been a valuable use of their time because it has not met either of their expectations.

To avoid unmet expectations and potential disappointment, we encourage new mentors and mentees to go "assumption hunting" in one of their early conversations. The best way to do this is straightforward: ask your mentoring partner what their assumptions are about mentoring and about the role of mentor and mentee. Then discuss your own assumptions and reach a mutual understanding about the purpose of mentoring in general and of each of your roles in this relationship.

» YOUR TURN «

1. What assumptions have you brought to prior mentoring/working relationships?

_____

_____

_____

_____

2. How did those affect the relationship?

_____

_____

_____

_____

3. What assumptions are you bringing with you into this mentoring relationship?

_____

_____

_____

_____

Determine Your Mutual Relationship Needs and Expectations

Once you have discussed your assumptions, it is time to switch focus to what you each expect and need from your mentoring relationship: what topics you might want to cover, what role you intend to play, and so on. You might reflect on how your expectations differ from or are similar to your assumptions and your mentoring partner's assumptions. Take the time now to reflect on this and answer the questions below. Use your answers as a guide in your conversation with your mentoring partner.

» YOUR TURN «

1. What I want from our mentoring relationship is:

_____

_____

_____

_____

2. What I intend to give to the mentoring relationship is:

_____

_____

_____

_____

3. What I expect from my mentoring partner is:

_____

_____

_____

_____

Let's check in with Aesha and Heather after each examined her needs and expectations about the mentoring relationship.

At their next meeting, Heather thanked Aesha for her text and told her that she was glad Aesha thought things were going so well. "So do I," responded Heather. She was trying to curb her tendency to launch into her story, so she waited for Aesha to begin. When Aesha remained silent, Heather said, "You said you wanted to talk about expectations, so why don't you dive right in?"

Aesha hesitated. "Maybe you should start," she said. Aesha had been brought up to be respectful and deferential. Interrupting, questioning, or contradicting anyone whom she considered senior or who held power and authority made her uncomfortable.

Therefore it was not surprising that she deferred to Heather, and Heather started talking.

Aesha took copious notes. She shuffled the pages in front of her, looked up, smiled, and nodded. Heather noted that Aesha seemed to be reluctant to add to the conversation. Did Aesha's silence mean she agreed with everything Heather was saying? Why didn't she jump in if she had questions? Heather had never met anyone like Aesha before and found her hard to read.

As Heather reflected on this for a moment, it occurred to her that she had not invited Aesha to share her ideas on what she expected from Heather as her mentor. She assumed that if Aesha had any questions she would volunteer them but it occurred to her that she would have to ask Aesha directly. "So, I've talked enough," Heather smiled, "what are your thoughts? I'd really like to know what you expect from me."

Although Aesha still didn't sense that Heather "got" her, she was relieved to be asked for her thoughts and was happy to share them. She left the meeting with a list of expectations and some ground rules and felt like she had contributed to the conversation. Heather had even given her an assignment: to come to the next meeting with some thoughts about her career goals.

This example demonstrates one of those areas in which cultural difference may be at play. As noted earlier, different cultures view boundaries differently. Like many in corporate America, Heather views boundaries as being specific, and she views the scope of her mentoring relationship to be limited to a specific domain: professional topics. For Aesha, whose orientation is more diffuse, it is not just appropriate but perhaps even expected for the mentoring relationship to spill over into other areas of her life.

Note that this is not necessarily an attribute of Aesha's ethnic heritage. There are often divergences in perspective and expectation on scope that vary based on gender, life stage, personality, and other elements of one's identity. For some people, having a mentoring relationship that extends beyond the work context may feel more like a need than an expectation. Perhaps, as it was for Aesha, there are pressing circumstances (her in-laws' visit) that created the need to extend the scope of the mentoring relationship. This could be a temporary or a permanent need. The important takeaway here is to notice where expectations and needs are for both mentoring partners and to create a shared understanding of how to address different expectations without judgment.

Discuss Learning and Development Goals

Our concept of mentoring is focused on the mentee's learning and developmental goals. It is important early on to set the stage for a relationship that will focus on learning and development. A focused discussion about learning goals increases trust and generates meaningful conversation. Rather than narrowing to particular goals, think of this conversation as one in which you are generating an expansive list of possible areas on which to focus. You can narrow this list later. Mentees should begin by reflecting on and discussing broad and open-ended questions such as the ones below with their mentors. If you need more time for reflection, ask for it.

» What are you really good at?

» What have been some of your biggest challenges?

» What do you want to get better at?

» What keeps you up at night when you think about your career?

Share your assumptions, expectations, and limitations candidly. To leverage your experience and expertise, it is necessary to take time to define desired learning outcomes. Table 6.1 has tips on this for both mentors and mentees.

» YOUR TURN «

Whether you are a mentor or mentee, make time to reflect upon and discuss these questions:

1. What are you really good at?

_____

_____

_____

_____

TABLE 6.1 *Tips for mentors and mentees*

Tips for mentors	Tips for mentees
» **At this stage in the relationship, many mentees are apprehensive about sharing vulnerabilities**. Allow the space for reflection and start with a conversation about strengths.	» **There is no right or wrong on learning and developmental goals.** Do not censor yourself as you enter this conversation. You may find that you want to learn about an area unrelated to your current role. This stage of the conversation is about creating an expansive list of possible goals.
» **New mentees are sometimes uneasy that they don't yet know what they want to be learning.** If this is true for your mentee, acknowledge the uneasiness, encourage exploration of possibilities, and revisit the conversation about goals periodically as themes emerge.	» **Remember that mentoring is a conversation.** Ask your mentor questions about their reactions and for suggestions of things that were helpful for them. Perhaps ask your mentor about what goals they set early in their relationship. What skills do you wish they had at your stage?
» **Resist the temptation to narrow the list to the goals you think are "a good idea" or "worthwhile."** In this stage you are still exploring options. You will narrow later.	

Source: Authors.

2. What is your biggest challenge?

_____

_____

_____

_____

3. What do you want to get better at?

_____

_____

_____

_____

4. What keeps you up at night when you think about your career?

_____

_____

_____

_____

Discuss Personality and Learning Styles

As you learn more about each other, you will want to talk about differences in your personalities and learning styles. You spent some time in Chapter 3 thinking about the way you process information and make decisions. Sharing this information with your mentoring partner will be helpful in several ways. When you have conversations about negotiating, as discussed in Chapter 7, you'll understand better how to reach agreement. As you set goals and work on them, you'll better understand how to create accountability, report progress, and celebrate achievements.

Earlier we discussed David Kolb's Learning Style Inventory, noting that Mia and Christopher had opposite learning styles. Mia wanted to get right to task, make quick decisions, and move forward, while Christopher wanted to understand context first. To feel comfortable working on goals, he wanted to begin by developing the relationship and taking things a bit more slowly. There is no right or wrong learning style (see Table 3.2 for examples of learning style descriptors). The key is to recognize your learning style and that of your partner, understand how those are similar or different, and adjust how you communicate with one another in a way that honors the style of each of you.

Learning style is not the only personality/learning difference to discuss, and you may be familiar with others. The Myers–Briggs Type Indicator (MBTI) is a popular and useful instrument that measures individuals' preferences on the following four continua:

1. *How you gather your energy.* This continuum specifies extraversion (E, drawing energy from action first) as one end point and introversion (I, gaining energy from time in reflection first) as the other.[54]

2. *How you gather information.* This continuum names sensing (S, trusting information that is tangible, concrete, and observed by senses) on one end and

intuition (N, tending to look more at a wider context, relying on theory and possibility) on the other.

3. *How you make decisions.* This continuum specifies thinking (T, making decisions in a more detached manner, based on logic, consistency, rules) on one end and feeling (F, making decisions based on association, consensus, and feelings of those involved, including their own) on the other.

4. *How you deal with structure and uncertainty.* This continuum places judging (J, preferring structure and needing decisions made) on one end and perceiving (P, preferring adaptability and flexibility) on the other.[55]

We likely see MBTI-type difference (referred to in four-letter acronyms) at play with Aesha and Heather. Heather, an ESTJ, prefers to talk to sort out her ideas. She has a high need for detail (S) and makes decisions based on how she thinks (T) instead of how she feels. Aesha, an INFJ, needs time to process and reflect (I), is focused more on concepts and theories (N), and makes decisions based on how she feels (F) rather than on how she thinks. Being aware of these differences will be critical to their success. But it is less important for them to know each other's MBTI type than it is for them to understand what the differences are between them and meet each other's needs.

For example, as someone who makes decisions based on whether she thinks they make sense, Heather does not have as much of a need to feel good with a goal in order to be committed to it. However, for Aesha it is important to note how she feels about a goal for it to be something she is motivated to achieve. Once Heather is aware of this, she can check in with Aesha to see how she feels about the goal, about her progress, and about the results she anticipates. Similarly, because Heather tends toward extraversion and Aesha tends toward introversion, it is important that they recognize and discuss this difference. Heather may want to process her thoughts in the mentoring meetings or sort through options by discussing them with Aesha. Aesha may want to process decisions alone and then discuss them with Heather after she has had time to reflect. Discussing this difference will help avoid misunderstanding and allow each of them the space to ask for what they need and the ability to identify what the other needs to make the most of their mentoring experience.

There are, of course, many other assessments that are useful in identifying personality and learning styles. Some pairs like to decide on an assessment that they will each complete and then discuss the results together. If you and your mentoring partner decide that this is an approach you would like to take, there are several tools you can choose from (see the appendix at the back of the book for resources). If you and your mentoring partner are in the same organization, check with your learning and development team to see if there is a preferred assessment used by your organization.

Taking an assessment can be useful in learning from differences because it can help you understand your mentoring partner better. Whether you take an assessment is up to you and your mentoring partner. Discussing your differences in personalities, preferences, styles, and learning from any assessment is far more important. Holding an open discussion about these differences allows you to structure your relationship in a way that honors each of you and helps you get to know each other in a deeper way. Table 6.2 offers some suggestions for getting ready for your initial conversation.

In addition, here are some useful questions to discuss in your initial mentoring meetings, to give yourself a chance to get to know one another's learning styles. If more questions occur to you as the conversation progresses, of course you should explore them.

» Do you need time to reflect on questions before discussing them?

» Will you need time to reflect on our mentoring discussions before making a decision about next action?

» Will you feel more comfortable or more constrained if we make an agenda or plan of action for our mentoring time together?

» When it comes to making decisions, do you prefer to do it based on what you think about the decision or how you feel about it?

» Do you need a lot of data to make decisions, or do you make them based more on a gut feeling?

Once you've gotten to know each other better, and have some idea of your learning styles, it is time to leverage what you've learned. In Part 3 of the book, we turn to the three remaining phases of the mentoring relationship: negotiating, facilitating, and coming to closure.

TABLE 6.2 *Getting ready: Initial conversation*

Agenda	Strategies for conversation	Questions to ponder
1. Take time to build trust and get to know each other.	Consider sending an introductory email before your first meeting.	What information might you exchange to get to know each other better? What points of connection have you discovered in your conversation? What else do you want to learn about each other?
2. Share guiding principles.	Share any truisms or words of wisdom with your mentoring partner that might help your partner get to know you better.	Is there a saying that you live by? What is the best advice that you have ever been given? Is there a mantra or motto to which you often turn?
3. Share career highlights and milestones.	Ask for a copy of your mentoring partner's bio in advance of the conversation. Ask your mentoring partner questions about their key experiences so you can learn their significance and value.	What is the meaning/lesson from each experience? What did you learn about yourself from each of your experiences?
4. Share mentoring stories.	Discuss previous mentoring experiences with your mentoring partner.	What did you like about your experiences? What did you each learn from your experiences? What would you like to carry forward into this relationship?
5. Share mentoring assumptions.	Talk about the mentoring assumptions and limitations you each bring to the relationship. Discuss implications for your relationship.	What assumptions do you hold about mentoring? What assumptions do you hold about the role of the mentor and mentee? What assumptions do you hold about each other and your relationship?

(continued)

TABLE 6.2 *Getting ready: Initial conversation (continued)*

Agenda	Strategies for conversation	Questions to ponder
6. Determine your mutual relationship needs and expectations.	Discuss your wants, needs, and expectations for the relationship.	What do you each want to get out of the mentoring relationship?
7. Begin to talk about the mentee's broad learning and development goals.	Have a conversation about the mentee's learning goals, desired outcomes, and the reasons they are important.	For mentees: What are you really good at? What is your biggest challenge? What do you want to get better at? What keeps you up at night when you think about your career?
8. Discuss personality and learning styles.	Talk about your individual learning styles or personality profiles.	How will you communicate with each other in a way that honors your differences?

Source: Adapted from Zachary, *The Mentor's Guide*, 124, Table 4.1.

Chapter Recap

1. Making a meaningful connection with your mentoring partner is the most critical element in laying a strong foundation for a mentoring partnership.

2. The time you have taken to lean forward into differences through self-reflection will help you learn more about your mentoring partner. To make a meaningful connection with your mentoring partner, you must be prepared to share your reflections with each other.

3. Unchecked assumptions can derail a mentoring relationship. To ensure that you and your mentoring partner are clear on your own roles, it is critical to determine the assumptions you hold about mentoring and about the roles of mentor and mentee before you meet with your mentoring partner. When you meet, check in with your partner to see if they are valid for them too.

4. Work toward good conversation that goes deeper. It's easy to fall back and get caught up in everyday work problems and challenges.

5. Good conversation is essential. The Levels of Conversation Model (see Figure 5.1) can help you determine where you are in your own conversations and self-correct as needed.

PART III

LEVERAGE DIFFERENCES

Meet Martin and Darren

Martin and Darren work at the US headquarters of ABC Company, a global manufacturer of medical devices. Darren, an African American male engineer, spent most of the past thirty years at ABC. Early in his career, he led the manufacturing function and now sits at the corporate headquarters along with the other members of the senior leadership team.

Darren sees mentoring as part of his responsibility as a leader. He has had many informal mentees in the past and, although he hadn't participated in any formal training, he considered himself "pretty successful" as a mentor. When the formal mentoring program for Young Professionals of Color (the YPC Mentoring Program) was released, Darren was totally on board. "I am excited by the energy and resources we are putting into it, and I definitely want to be part of it," he told the program coordinator.

Martin moved from Mexico to the United States with his family when he was five years old. Now, at age twenty-six, he has been at ABC for three years and is a line lead in the manufacturing department. His coworkers seek his advice and enjoy working with him. Martin was excited to be paired with someone as influential and respected as Darren. Martin thought that this mentoring relationship might be just the ticket he'd been waiting for to get his voice heard. Manufacturing had been great for Martin as he worked his way through school, and now he was eager to move out of manufacturing and be noticed by senior leadership. Martin believed he could accomplish big things but was not sure what they might be.

SEVEN

Establishing Agreements

The second phase of our mentoring model is *negotiating* (see Figure 1.1). In this chapter we'll explore what it means to negotiate the framework of your mentoring relationship in the context of cultural differences. "Negotiating" may seem like a strong word to use in relation to the softer term "mentoring," but the reality is that mentors and mentees need to establish agreements together to set the parameters of the relationship. The negotiation process is not about a mentor proclaiming their desired practice and the mentee accepting it; nor is it about offering terms and counterterms. Rather, effective negotiation requires mentor and mentee to discuss, adapt, and adopt the parameters that will govern the relationship. Essentially, the negotiation phase gives mentoring partners the time and permission they need to cocreate a relationship that works for both people and that will keep them on track throughout their mentoring relationship.

The negotiation process takes into account the needs, cultural backgrounds, learning styles, and preferences of all parties involved in the mentoring relationship. The dynamics of negotiation must consider the differences between partners in outlook, background, culture, power, and identity. This is why it is critical to begin by spending time learning about each other. According to psychologist Andy Molinsky, writing in *Global Dexterity*, when you are working closely with someone from a different culture, each person's cultural code for behavior will likely differ along the following six dimensions:

1. Directness (how straightforward you can be).

2. Enthusiasm (how much positive emotion and energy you can show).

3. Formality (how much deference and respect you are expected to demonstrate in this situation).

4. Assertiveness (how strongly you may express your voice).

5. Self-promotion (how positively you can speak about your skills and accomplishments).

6. Personal disclosure (how much you can reveal about yourself).[56]

Understanding where each partner in the mentoring relationship falls on these dimensions is critical. After you spend time building trust and getting to know each other, you'll be more familiar with your own and your mentoring partner's comfort in each of these categories, you'll be more able to notice when your approach differs from your partner's preference, and you can figure out when and how to adapt in a way that is both comfortable for you and authentic for you. Molinsky notes that people often hold on to a false belief that there is one appropriate way to behave. Instead, appropriate behavior falls within a range, which he calls the "zone of appropriateness."[57] The "right" behavior is actually a range of behavior that lies both in your personal comfort zone and in the zone of appropriateness.[58]

The negotiating process requires mentoring partners to set the parameters of their relationship within the zone of appropriateness. This includes three steps: (1) clarifying mentoring expectations, (2) establishing accountability assurances, and (3) setting well-defined goals. Each step builds on the work you did previously in getting to know each other. Now you can use this knowledge to set expectations and to enable your growth and development. Successful negotiation results in a work plan that helps direct, focus, and maximize your mentoring time.

Step 1. Clarifying Mentoring Expectations

Mentoring expectations are linked to assumptions we make about our roles and responsibilities (see Chapter 5). These assumptions are especially critical to understand and keep in mind during this step, when you are clarifying who is going to be responsible for what in the relationship. Here's how this played out for Darren and Martin.

Darren was surprised when he received a call from Martin just a few days after the mentoring program kickoff. He hadn't planned on calling him to schedule time to meet until the following week. But Martin was eager to get started and said that he had lots of questions, so they agreed to meet after work in the café next to the office.

Martin dove right in with questions about work and the company, and the questions continued during their meal. Clearly, he was fired up and ready for change. Darren was glad to see Martin's enthusiasm and that he had come prepared with questions, but he could tell it was going to take some work to manage Martin's expectations.

Darren could see that Martin had plenty of drive and ambition and was passionate about making things better, and he was impressed with how well Martin listened and related to him. But as Martin explained that he was looking for a mentor to gain exposure, increase his visibility, and define a pathway to promotion, Darren was taken aback. He couldn't recall ever feeling the need for a mentoring relationship to increase his exposure. He had assumed that Martin's motivation for mentoring was simply to have someone to ask about how to succeed at ABC. The whole idea seemed strange to Darren, and he needed to find out more about how Martin expected him to help.

"Martin," said Darren, "you've really thought this through. But I'm realizing that we haven't talked yet about what we expect from each other in mentoring. Let's pull back a little. I want to make sure that I'm clear about my own role and what I can do for you." Darren also wanted to make sure that Martin understood that he was not going to be his fixer, his sponsor, or his complaint department. Plus, Darren wasn't sure he could deliver on Martin's expectation that Darren would get him a new role at ABC.

"Tell me a little more about what's driving you," said Darren.

"I've got to find a way out of manufacturing," said Martin. "I'm hoping that you can help get me out of there and find something bigger."

"That might happen as a result of our mentoring," Darren responded, "but I don't think it should necessarily be our target. I want to be a sounding board for you, to coach you on your goals, and to help you gain perspective. If it's needed, I can introduce you to people who might be able to help you get your next role. But I just want to be really clear that I can't promise you a promotion and I don't see my role as getting you promoted. I think of my role as helping you become promotable. I can help you think about what you do well, what you could do better, and what skills you might need to get to the next step. How does that sound?"

Martin admitted that was a little disappointing, but that it seemed reasonable. If Darren couldn't get him a promotion, who could? Martin wasn't sure how he would get where he wanted to go in his career, but it certainly couldn't hurt to have an ally like

Darren. The conversation then turned to what the pair could agree was Martin's role as mentee.

» YOUR TURN «

1. What can you and your mentoring partner agree is the role of the mentor in your relationship?

_____

_____

_____

_____

2. What can you and your mentoring partner agree is the role of the mentee in your relationship?

_____

_____

_____

_____

3. What is your mutual expectation about what can happen as a result of mentoring?

_____

_____

_____

_____

Step 2. Establishing Accountability Assurances

Once you and your mentoring partner have surfaced your individual assumptions about the roles of a mentor and a mentee, you can create accountability assurances to manage and set expectations. At this point you may feel like this is an unnecessary step that adds undue formality to the relationship; or you may feel that it goes against a preference for organic connection or lack of structure. And yet—particularly in the context of cross-cultural relationships—these accountability assurances are key to keeping your relationship on track, meeting expectations, managing conflict, and overcoming obstacles during the course of your mentoring relationship. Accountability assurances set a framework for your mentoring relationship that create role clarity and guide your mentoring partner how to communicate with you.

Time and again, we have helped troubled mentoring relationships get back on track by coaching mentors and mentees to revisit the agreements they set with their mentoring partners at the beginning of their relationship. When we ask successful mentoring pairs what the key ingredient to their success was, they often cite the frank, open conversations they had with their mentoring partners about setting agreements as the rudder that kept their subsequent relationship focused and directed.

Setting accountability assurances helps create mutual accountability for the mentoring relationship, so that both the mentor and the mentee understand each other's roles and preferences. When there is ambiguity in the mentoring framework, there is a higher likelihood that the mentor or mentee will walk away disappointed or confused. For example, mentoring partners who missed this step tell us that they hadn't met in quite a while because each person was waiting for the other to reach out to schedule the next meeting. Accountability assurances enable mentoring partners to stay in conversation because they have an objective agreement that keeps them on track. Accountability assurances become a reference point to answer questions about original intent and structure. Mentoring is, after all, based on mutual accountability.

The key is to use your cultural competence to define accountability assurances in such a way that they are culturally relevant and responsive. This means making sure that what you both agree to is mutually understood and appropriate to your mentoring partner and their culture, and is not based on your cultural assumptions. The accountability conversation has four components that ensure mutual accountability: ground rules, confidentiality, boundaries, and emotional triggers. We encourage you to have this conversation with your mentoring partner and do it early in the relationship. If you skip it, you may find yourselves backtracking to stay on course. Let's look at each component in depth.

Ground Rules

The first step in setting accountability assurances is to establish ground rules for your relationship. These include such topics as the following:

» How often are we going to meet and for how long?

» Where are we going to meet?

» What happens if we have to reschedule?

» Who sets the agenda? What is included on the agenda? When does it get sent out? Is there an opportunity for feedback on the agenda?

» Will we summarize what we've learned? When? (At the end of the meeting, in a follow-up email?)

» How will we end each meeting? Will we each have a to-do list?

» What are our expectations about preparing for our mentoring meeting? What does it mean to be "prepared"?[59]

Let's see how Darren and Martin handled this step.

A few weeks later, Darren felt that conversation was flowing easily with Martin, and they had made progress in getting to know each other. Darren approached the subject of establishing agreements. "Martin, it's time to set some ground rules for our relationship. Where would you like to start?"

Martin felt like a deer in headlights, staring at Darren as he sat behind his big desk. He appreciated Darren asking what ground rules he wanted, but he felt like he was being disrespectful to Darren by starting off with what he wanted. It was a long way from manufacturing to the executive suite. Martin was quiet for about a minute, which felt to him like an eternity, and then he shifted uncomfortably in his seat. "I don't know where to start," he said. "Maybe tell me what ground rules you set with your team."

Darren paused, curious about the discomfort he was seeing in Martin. He was surprised by it, since Martin had seemed so at ease at dinner the last time they met. Now, when they were talking about how to formulate ground rules about their relationship, Martin was reluctant to contribute. Darren dove in, trying to alleviate some of the discomfort that seemed to have suddenly overtaken Martin. In a few moments, Martin relaxed, but both Darren and Martin realized that they needed to spend a bit more time figuring out how to leverage their cultural differences about power.

What happened here? By asking Martin to start on agreement setting, Darren's intention was to neutralize some of the power imbalance that he was certain might otherwise cause too much formality in the relationship. He was trying to communicate to Martin that he had as much say in setting agreements as Darren did. Darren wanted Martin to know that he wasn't going to unilaterally implement the structure and rules that worked for him. However, Martin, sitting in Darren's office and being asked by Darren, a senior executive behind a big desk, to suggest boundaries and ground rules for their relationship, couldn't overcome the cultural subtext that it would be presumptive and disrespectful of authority for him to state the parameters of their relationship.

You can see from this example how setting ground rules up front can help neutralize power imbalances and set the stage for effective learning. The key here is for mentor and mentee to approach this discussion with the shared understanding that they are cocreating the framework of the relationship. And given inherent (implicit) power dynamics, often the mentor must, as Darren did, take extra steps to point out the expectation that the mentee will play as much of a role in forming the parameters of the relationship. Despite Darren's intention, however, it is most effective for the mentor to be explicit in this expectation and to discuss with the mentee what might be needed to overcome any hesitancy to partner and even creatively to preemptively suggest possibilities. For example, Darren might address the power differential simply by suggesting they move the meeting to the conference table in his office or meeting in a quiet corner in the cafeteria.

In setting ground rules, keep Molinsky's framework in mind and look for a "zone of appropriateness" where the mentor's and mentee's cultural expectations and comfort zones overlap so that each partner can express their expectations and come to an agreement about what behavior is "in the zone." Let's return to Darren and Martin to see how else this might play out in setting ground rules.

Through his own self-reflection on how he best made decisions and learned, Darren realized that he most identified with the assimilating learning style—he processes information internally, gathering lots of data and insight, sharing his thoughts only once he has reached a decision or is close to it. For his part, Martin has more of an accommodating learning style. He processes things by talking them out and likes to try things to see if they work.

Once Darren and Martin learned this about each other, they were able to have a conversation about how to make this work for them in their mentoring relationship.

"As we talked about a few weeks ago," Martin told Darren, "I really need to be able to bounce ideas off you and see how they will stick. I find if I do this with my managers, they think I'm all over the place, or that I'm being presumptuous, but I know you're more of a thinker—a data guy. What's the best way to do this without driving you crazy?"

Darren was grateful that Martin was raising this issue. He had anticipated this might be an obstacle and hadn't been sure how to bring it up. "Well, what if you tee up an issue with what your need is? If you just need a sounding board, you can say so. And if we have an agenda with time limits, it might help me rein it in if we get too far afield. Also, I hope you'll understand if I ask a bunch of questions and, if you are looking for my opinion or a recommendation, maybe we can agree that you'll allow me to process for a bit after our meeting and follow up with you with a call or an email once I've thought it through."

Darren also had an issue he wanted to raise, and he figured this probably was a good time to do it. "After all these years in management, I've become a low context guy. It's how our team usually communicates in meetings and I find it helps us focus. I like data and everything, but it really helps me to understand things if we can start with some kind of executive summary. It doesn't have to be written, but it would be helpful if you can. The point is that if you have a concern or an issue, I think we can tackle it best if you've thought through it a bit ahead of time and then you sum it up for me. With more questions and discussion, we can get to the issue better."

Martin was struck by what Darren said. This framework of "low context" was new to him but he understood. "This is already a bit of an awakening about why my manager gets irritated with me. I'm kind of the opposite. Maybe that makes me 'high context'?" I like to understand why and what happened and how people feel about something. I'm happy to do an executive summary, and I know you'll do the same, but I'm hoping you'll understand if I've got some questions around things."

With that discussion, Darren and Martin began to set some ground rules. Martin would set an agenda for each meeting and schedule some time to think through how to summarize his particular issue for Darren. Darren would give as much detail as he could to Martin, and Martin would try to remember to ask for it if he needed it. When Martin was looking for Darren's opinion on something, he would understand if Darren asked questions of his own, took the time to process, and then followed up in an email. Darren would commit to getting back to Martin within a week from the discussion and not take too much time thinking it through.

» YOUR TURN «

1. What ground rules might you use in your mentoring relationship?

_____

_____

_____

_____

2. What potential challenges do you see in setting ground rules?

_____

_____

_____

_____

3. How are you and your mentoring partner going to hold yourselves accountable for honoring your ground rules?

_____

_____

_____

_____

Confidentiality

When we approach the subject of confidentiality at our trainings, if the training is in North America, inevitably someone suggests that they should apply the "Vegas Rule"—"What happens in Vegas, stays in Vegas"—to their mentoring relationship:

"What happens in our mentoring relationship, stays in our mentoring relationship." Our response is always the same: it's not that simple.

An effective confidentiality agreement must encourage sharing while also creating psychological safety. Confidentiality cannot exist unless there is already trust in the relationship, which is yet another reason that mentoring partners must take the time to get to know each other before establishing accountability assurances. True confidentiality depends on each person feeling a sense of psychological safety. This means that both mentoring partners must feel that their confidentiality agreement is sufficient to create a safe space for sharing—and that is different for each person. The key is to find the "zone of appropriateness" that overlaps the mentor's cultural code and the mentee's cultural code.

Recall Molinsky's dimensions of a cultural code of behavior mentioned at the beginning of this chapter. Mentor and mentee each bring a cultural code about how much emotion they feel comfortable sharing, how much they can self-promote, and how much they can reveal. Mentoring partners will likely discuss the mentee's strengths and weaknesses, yet the mentor may be in a position to influence (whether directly or indirectly) the mentee's compensation. Mentors may be on a leadership team with their mentee's supervisor. There may be information shared that influences the business or potential business strategy. Perhaps a mentor may find themselves in a position to advocate for the mentee without the mentee's knowledge. All these possibilities must be discussed, and a solution that balances safety concerns, business needs, and cultural comfort with disclosure must be reached.

Here's how confidentiality played out for Darren and Martin.

As Darren learned more about Martin's work environment, he saw several opportunities for ABC to make improvements in the processes for quality control in the manufacturing department. On his commute home, Darren had a monthly check-in with one of his peers, Charla, who supervised the company VP's manufacturing division, among other teams. Darren was tempted to let Charla know of these opportunities for improvement and felt he had a duty to do so, but he was afraid that if he did so now, he would have to reveal some of the information Martin shared with him in confidence.

Darren wrapped up his check-in with Charla early and debated whether to fill the remaining minutes with a heads-up about the process improvements. "I'd better not," he thought, as his confidentiality agreement with Martin was to let Martin know in advance if he wanted to share anything they had discussed. Darren and Martin had just started to make headway, and he didn't want to jeopardize the trust they were building. Darren made a mental note to find out if Martin would be comfortable with Darren sharing information before his next check-in with Charla.

» YOUR TURN «

1. What does confidentiality mean to you?

_____

_____

_____

_____

2. What safeguards would you want to put in place to assure your mentoring conversations remain confidential?

_____

_____

_____

_____

Boundaries

The next accountability assurance focuses on setting the scope of the mentoring relationship—that is, boundaries. Although it can be a challenging conversation, engaging in a discussion about boundaries with your mentoring partner is essential. In Chapter 3 we discussed how one of the factors that varies by culture is the degree to which we engage each other in specific areas of our lives or diffusely in multiple areas of our lives.[60] In specific cultures appropriateness depends highly on context and role. In diffuse cultures, where "everything is connected to everything," it is impossible to distinguish one's professional role from one's personal role or role in the community.[61]

We saw how this played out for Aesha and Heather. Heather's expectation, which is typical of those from a more specific culture, was that she would mentor Aesha only on work-related matters. Aesha had a very different expectation. She wanted to address her ability to manage life and work. Only when Aesha and Heather discussed the roots and importance of this need were they able to come to an agreement about boundaries in their relationship in a way that met Aesha's needs to talk about integrating work and life and Heather's needs to keep mentoring focused on Aesha's professional success.

As it was for Aesha and Heather, expectations of boundaries often differ by age, generation, gender, life experience, life stage, and a variety of other factors. Two primary types of boundaries may be relevant in mentoring relationships: boundaries on time and availability, and boundaries on scope of mentoring topics.

Boundaries on time and availability: These are boundaries about when you are comfortable communicating with your mentoring partner. Questions to consider include the following:

» Will I respond or reach out to my mentoring partner on evenings or weekends?

» Am I available while on vacation?

» Will I be available for my mentoring partner to just swing by my office/ workspace? If not, what happens if I want to meet at a time not previously scheduled?

» Do I prefer texts, emails, or phone calls?

» How quickly can my mentoring partner expect me to respond?

Boundaries on scope of mentoring topics: Questions to consider include the following:

» Will we talk about only work-related topics?

» Will we talk about development unrelated to my job?

» Will we discuss issues that are related to my personal life or my community involvement? If so, what are the boundaries and limitations to that discussion?

» What happens if you raise a topic that I am not comfortable with?

» How comfortable am I with using the mentoring time for "venting"?

In our workshops we dedicate time for our participants to identify and share boundaries. Here are some examples of boundaries mentoring partners set regarding addressing daily work problems, scope of mentoring, and time and availability.

1. Addressing daily work problems.

   » We are not going to spend time talking about day-to-day work problems and crises.

   » We will address daily work problems and crises at each meeting but will set a ten-minute limit to address daily work problems.

   » If we need to address daily work problems, we will, but we want to be careful to keep our learning goals as the main item on our agenda.

2. Scope of mentoring.

   » We are not going to focus on getting a promotion.

   » We will talk about work-life and community issues as they relate to the mentee's ability to achieve their goals.

   » We will focus on the capabilities you need to develop to realize your goals.

3. Time and availability.

   » If you need me urgently, send me a text and I'll send you some available times.

   » I have to leave early on Fridays and switch into family obligations, so please don't expect a response until Monday.

   » Feel free to drop by if I'm in the office but understand that if I can't talk then we will schedule time.

Emotional Triggers

We used to talk about emotional triggers as hot buttons, but lately we've received lots of pushback on this term. It seems that even the term "hot button" is a hot button! And it is culturally relative. Now we refer to them as *triggers*. Marshall Goldsmith wrote a whole book on the topic of triggers, and so we will go with his definition: "A behavior trigger is any stimulus that impacts our behavior."[62] This definition is admittedly broad, and certainly its application is not limited to mentoring. We raise it here because part of leveraging difference in mentoring is cocreating a relationship that manages our triggers. Although triggers are often thought of as negative, they can be positive as well. The key to managing negative triggers is to articulate them early on. It will help your mentoring partner understand which triggers to avoid and which triggers to leverage.

In Chapter 3 we offered tips for identifying motivating factors. These can be thought of as positive triggers. We suggest that you and your mentoring partner talk about negative triggers, those that evoke irritation, frustration, or an unproductive emotional reaction in you, like shutting down or getting angry. Be specific about your triggers. If being late is a trigger for you, what do you mean by "late"? In some cultures, arriving within fifteen minutes of the start time is expected. In others, anything after five minutes might be late. In still others, if the meeting occurs within the hour in which it was scheduled, it is not considered late. In our work with global clients we've seen that early clarification around the trigger of what is "late" can make a big difference in avoiding future conflict.

There are other triggers as well. Here are two of ours. Coauthor Lois is a stickler for follow-through. When people make promises and don't deliver in the time frame to which they committed, it really riles her. She manages this trigger in mentoring relationships by asking her mentees to communicate with her in between meetings if they won't be able to follow through on something. Coauthor Lisa gets triggered when someone sends her an email about something and then texts or leaves a voicemail "just as a backup." This "belt and suspenders" approach feels intrusive to Lisa. She asks her colleagues to mark an email with a high-priority flag to avoid this trigger.

» YOUR TURN «

1. What are your personal boundary issues?

_____

_____

_____

_____

2. What cultural boundaries might you face in a mentoring relationship?

_____

_____

_____

_____

3. What are your negative triggers? What behaviors can your mentoring partner take to avoid them?

_____

_____

_____

_____

4. What strategies might you put in place to prevent you and your mentoring partner from crossing boundaries and pushing each other's triggers?

_____

_____

_____

_____

Step 3: Setting Well-Defined Goals

Learning is the focus and the litmus test for an effective mentoring relationship. If no learning is taking place, then the relationship is not a mentoring relationship. Learning in a mentoring relationship is reciprocal, but the focus of the learning must be centered on mutually defined goals for a mentee's learning and development. Successful mentoring depends on successful goal setting. Therefore, the goal-setting process is key to creating the strong foundation necessary to achieve positive results during the mentoring relationship. Earlier, during the preparation phase of the mentoring relationship, you and your mentoring partner talked about goals in broad terms. Now, in this phase, goals become more clearly articulated and success criteria are defined.

Starter Goals

A goal first presents itself as a *starter goal*. Starter goals emerge from initial discussions about the results a mentee might like to see, and at this point they can often be vague, broad, and unspecific. They beg for further exploration and specificity before they can become measurable and actionable (we'll discuss the concept of SMART goals in depth near the end of this chapter). Let's look at Darren and Martin's starter goals.

Once Darren and Martin understood each other's roles in the mentoring relationship, they began to brainstorm a list of outcomes that might help Martin get closer to his goal of moving out of manufacturing. It all seemed a bit fuzzy, but a few ideas started to emerge.

> » Improve relationships with upper management.
> » Get better at influencing my upper management.
> » Move somewhere else at ABC where I could learn more.
> » Help my team develop.

This was a good list of starter goals, thought Darren. He put a note in his mentoring journal to spend some time with Martin helping him set a vision.

We'll speak more about setting a vision in Chapter 8.

» YOUR TURN «

1. At the end of your mentoring relationship, what skills do you or does your mentee or mentor want to have?

   _____

   _____

   _____

   _____

2. What kind of leader do you or does your mentee want to be?

_____

_____

_____

_____

3. What do you or does your mentee want to be able to do differently once your mentoring relationship is over?

_____

_____

_____

_____

Sleeper Goals

Often, while working on goals, *sleeper goals* emerge. These less-conscious goals weren't initially uncovered. As the mentoring relationship progresses, however, these goals tend to surface and become new priorities. Darren and Martin provide a good example of how this happens.

As Darren and Martin started to refine Martin's starter goal of moving out of manufacturing, Darren asked Martin what he thought his strengths were. Martin found he couldn't answer the question. With further discussion, Darren and Martin realized that Martin couldn't decide what he wanted to do next until he understood what he did well. A sleeper goal emerged for Martin: "Discover my strengths."

Soon, another sleeper goal emerged. As Martin was working on helping his team develop, he realized that he needed to figure out how to better delegate. This had been a long-standing yet unaddressed issue. Now, however, it was clear to Darren that Martin would not be able to move forward until this issue was resolved.

Sleeper goals are goals that have been there all along, just not explicitly acknowledged. Once they surface, sleeper goals are no longer sleeping. Now they are compelling and require action.

Make Goals Outcome-Based, Not Performance-Based

Here's a tip that will help you make the most of the mentoring time and the goal-setting process, and develop the skill of curiosity we discussed earlier in this book: cultivate curiosity by developing learning goals instead of performance goals.[63] Beware of the temptation to develop performance-based goals. Many mentoring pairs choose a goal for the mentee that is already a part of a mentee's performance expectation. This is a missed opportunity to leverage the power of mentoring to advance a mentee's learning and development. Instead, we encourage you to find an outcome-based goal.

An outcome-based goal is set around the desired outcome of mentoring. It should answer one of the following questions:

» What do I need to know in order to accomplish my goal?

» What skills do I need to acquire?

» What do I want to be different as a result of the mentoring relationship?

» What am I currently good at that I want to build on?

» What am I currently not good at that I want to get better at?

We do not mean to suggest that mentoring pairs shouldn't discuss strategies to improve performance. However, discussions about a mentee's performance should be limited and focus more on *how* to do things rather than *what* to do. Mentoring is not remedial, it is developmental. When you use mentoring time to focus solely on how to better perform your job, it is a missed opportunity. Mentoring time is often the only dedicated space for mentees to focus on their growth. Let's explore how this played out for Aesha and Heather.

The first time Aesha and Heather met to negotiate goals, Heather said, "Aesha, I'd like to see you exceed metrics in your annual review. Just good is not good enough. You have to be so good that no one can deny your competency. Hit your numbers out of the park. How is your success measured by your manager? Let's set some goals around your performance metrics."

At Heather's suggestion, Aesha brought a copy of her annual performance goals. They brainstormed six ways that Aesha could "hit it out of the park." As Aesha closed her notebook, she felt a bit disappointed. She was already going to "hit it out of the park." And these goals didn't really excite her. Heather saw the look on her face and asked, "What's wrong?"

"To be honest," said Aesha, "I'm not that motivated by these goals. I'm going to do a good job at my current job. I'm worried I won't be using our time wisely if we only set goals around what I'm already supposed to be doing. I'd love to set some goals around how I can learn new things and grow."

Heather was a bit surprised—she had always been motivated by the bonus that came when she overdelivered. She reminded herself that she needed to keep in mind that she and Aesha were motivated by completely different things. Heather remembered what she had learned about Aesha and her desire to become a better leader. "All right," she said, "let's course correct. At our next session, come prepared with some things you want to learn that do excite you, and we will refine these further."

Aesha smiled as she wrote down this assignment. Heather had to admit that she was learning some things about mentoring while getting to know Aesha, and she started the next meeting mindful of this wisdom. For Aesha, the main thing was to grow and to achieve balance. Any goals had to incorporate Aesha's criteria for success, not just Heather's. Together, they changed Aesha's starter goals. Now they were: "Become proficient in three of the competencies of a product analyst: strategic thinking, time management, and communication."

SMART Goals

Before you move forward, set aside time to convert your broad goals or starter goals into SMART goals. SMART is an acronym for goals that are specific, measurable, action-oriented, realistic, and timely.[64] Mentors can facilitate the process by encouraging the mentee to choose a goal that is a *stretch goal*—a goal that will make a difference in a mentee's abilities, skills, and capabilities. Remember that you are each approaching the mentoring relationship with your own unique views on success, motivation, and ideal performance. Setting SMART goals allows mentor and mentee to clarify how you will measure success and create goals that are personalized and meaningful. Both mentor and mentee must be invested in, and clear on, the desired outcomes.

SMART goals must be well-defined. They must meet certain criteria in order to produce positive learning outcomes. In our experience SMART goal setting is a challenge for both mentors and mentees. It isn't business as usual. Nor should it be. The conversation that leads to setting goals is critical in so many ways, not just to the outcome but also to the relationship. Let's see how Aesha and Heather turned Aesha's starter goals into SMART goals.

Starter goal: Become proficient in three of the competencies of a product analyst: strategic thinking, time management, and communication.

SMART goals:

Strategic thinking: Develop my competency in strategic thinking so that I demonstrate the skills and apply the steps needed to implement an initiative at Any Healthcare (specific). By the end of the mentoring period (timely), I will develop a marketing investment strategy that will define paid and unpaid media activities and produce a return on investment greater than 1.0 (action-oriented, measurable), and solicit and incorporate feedback from three directors (realistic).

Time management: Improve my skills at time management so I can better balance home and family obligations (action-oriented). By the time my in-laws arrive (timely), I'll have identified and scheduled my recurring tasks, and determined what I can let go of and what I can delegate (specific, measurable). I will have the right tools in place to help me manage my time (realistic).

Communication: Understand what is considered effective communication at Any Healthcare. By my next annual performance review (timely), I will have reviewed three successful marketing annual operating plans and met with the VP of communication (specific, measurable, action-oriented, realistic) so that I can understand Any Healthcare's protocol and best practices.

» YOUR TURN «

1. Create a SMART mentoring learning goal.

_____

_____

_____

_____

2. List five ways you will measure your success.

_____

_____

_____

_____

3. What will be different once you complete your goal?

_____

_____

_____

_____

Create a Work Plan

Your mentoring agreement will come from the work you have done to clarify mentoring expectations, establish accountability assurances, and set goals. Even if formalizing it into a written agreement seems too much for you, we urge you to at least take notes so you can recall your agreements at any time. Next, you need to create a work plan for achieving each of the goals you have agreed on. Use your work plan to get started and to see your mentoring agreement through to its completion. This will ensure you keep moving forward. If you don't make a work plan, you will wish you had!

Here's how to do it: Itemize your learning goals, success criteria, and objectives for each goal. Lay out the specific steps you need to take to move forward. Set a date for completion for each goal and include check-in dates (more about that in Chapter 8). We take Donald Berwick's sage advice to heart: "Some is not a number; soon is not a time."[65] Make your work plan work for you. Put it in writing and be specific.

Now that you know your mentoring partner better and have established agreements for your mentoring relationship, the real learning begins. In the next chapter, we'll dive into enabling growth, the heart of the mentoring process.

━━━━━━━━━━ **Chapter Recap** ━━━━━━━━━━

1. Make accountability assurances (agreements around ground rules, confidentiality boundaries, and negative triggers) that are culturally relevant and meaningful for both you and your mentoring partner. This will provide an essential guardrail to keep your relationship on track. Don't assume cultural relevance! Talk about the assurances *before* you sign off on them.

2. Effective mentoring is dependent upon setting SMART goals: learning-based goals that are specific, measurable, action-oriented, realistic, and timely.

3. Once goals are set, mentoring partners must make a work plan so that they can gauge progress and stay accountable. It is helpful to set dates to monitor progress that update the work plan until the goal is completed.

EIGHT

Enabling Growth

Enabling growth is the longest of the four phases, the heart of mentoring, and by far the most exciting and challenging work you will do together. The preparation you've been working so hard on—to this point, preparing yourselves, and then setting the parameters of your mentoring relationship—position you and your partner for success.

This next phase offers a tremendous opportunity for learning and development, yet it is also when mentoring partnerships become most vulnerable to derailment because it requires the biggest investment of time, energy, and sustained momentum in order to see results. Mentorship is a living, evolving relationship. Keep it fresh and moving forward by continually monitoring your progress and celebrating learning milestones to create the momentum you need to successfully accomplish your mentoring goals.

Early on, Martin was struggling with how to explain the way his family's story had guided him and why he felt that getting where he wanted was going to be such a struggle. As it turned out, Darren made it easy for him. At their next meeting, Darren asked Martin if he'd given any more thought as to why he was so doubtful about his capabilities. This time Martin didn't hesitate in responding.

Martin told Darren that he had been receiving a lot of flak lately from management. "They appreciate that I hit my numbers. They really do. They've told me so. But every time I offer suggestions or ask questions about how we can improve processes and procedures, I get pushback. In fact, they seem irritated."

Darren probed for more specific examples. Martin told him that he had suggested a new spreadsheet for tracking productivity at a recent team meeting. Several managers were obviously annoyed and told him that he was being insubordinate by not following the proven procedures they had laid out for him. Martin's intent had been to identify a more efficient way, not to disregard established procedure, but he hadn't been given a chance to say so. Darren understood why Martin would be upset. Maybe Martin was resenting what he felt were arbitrary rules that were designed to keep him quiet.

Martin continued. "And there's more—the performance improvement plan that my manager put me on. Frankly, I'm embarrassed to talk about it. It upset me when I got it and I'm still upset about it." It was clear Martin felt he had been evaluated unfairly, and the items he had been dinged on were things he couldn't do anything about. Working in manufacturing had been great for Martin as he worked his way through school, but he knew he could contribute more and was ready to prove himself in a new challenge. Martin felt he could accomplish bigger things but was not sure what they might be. Now he was worried that he would never be able to move out of manufacturing. He couldn't see a path out and felt like he was being kept down in a position that was beneath his ability, and maybe now he was even being forced out.

Getting Unstuck

Martin was stuck and Darren was stymied. Why Martin was stuck remained a mystery. Martin seemed to have a fixed mindset (see Chapter 2) about the possibility for change. Darren didn't have any idea how to direct Martin, and he certainly couldn't just tell Martin to figure it out himself. Darren knew he had authority to communicate directly with plant leaders on Martin's behalf, but should he? How could he best facilitate Martin's growth and development? He found himself stuck too.

Darren wanted to be supportive, but first he needed to understand where Martin was coming from. What was he missing? Darren wanted to know what it was like for Martin on a day-to-day basis, and what "arbitrary rules" were holding him back and in what ways. What was keeping Martin from raising concerns with his supervisor? What was it that Martin really wanted to do anyway?

As Darren got curious about Martin's thinking, he knew that he needed more information to understand who Martin was and what truly motivated him. He wondered whether Martin's motivation and capabilities were really aligned. One way Darren could help Martin get unstuck was to help Martin see how he could grow, and how he could take ownership of his work situation. But in order to do this, Darren needed to have a sense of where Martin should focus his energies. One concept that might have helped speed the process for Darren is something called *native genius*.

Working with Native Genius

In the book *Multipliers*, Liz Wiseman defines "native genius" as "something that people do, not only exceptionally well, but absolutely naturally." She explains: "They do it easily (without extra effort) and freely (without condition).... They get results that are head-and-shoulders above others, but they do it without breaking a sweat."[66] We've found this concept particularly helpful in assisting the mentors we work with. In a very real sense, good mentoring *is* genius making. When mentors are able to help their mentees identify their native genius, understand it, and cultivate it, transformation happens. Kristen Wheeler, founder and creator of the Native Genius Method, describes native genius this way:

> [It is] the meeting of what you're good at and what you enjoy doing. What's even more important is that Native Genius consists of actions you do on autopilot that you may not realize you're doing—that's the "native" part. The "genius" part is that others are noticing and valuing those actions because they're above and beyond. Others are impacted by the special, shimmery quality of your Native Genius Actions. However, because these actions are on autopilot for you, you likely feel them as quite ordinary and think that anyone could do them. You may not even notice that you're doing them at all! This is why most of us tend to overlook and undervalue our own Native Geniuses. We also underestimate how good we are at them. Then we discount them further because we enjoy them, especially if we've learned that "real work" shouldn't feel good.[67]

When we step into our own native genius, we position ourselves for growth. We start looking for opportunities that allow us to repeat the behaviors that capitalize on our motivation and competence. We get better at what we do and get better results. Here's how Darren helped Martin identify his native genius.

Darren decided to ask Martin some probing questions to help identify where Martin's native genius lay. He asked, What do you like to do at work? What do you think you do best at work? When are you at your easiest, freest, and most productive? What drags you down?

In response to Darren's questions, Martin started to describe the things in his job he thought he did best. "Well," he said, "I am really good at holding my team accountable to metrics even though it's not my favorite thing. It drains me to follow procedures that I don't think are efficient, but if you give me a goal, I'll hit it."

"What else?" Darren could see that Martin had something percolating.

Martin smiled. "I do love finding new ways to motivate my team. I can read people fairly well and see what is going to get them to do the job well. We have team meetings every Monday, where we share stories and successes, and I always have a fun little game or something. I spend a bunch of time on the weekend thinking through what I'll do with them on Monday. And on Sunday nights, I look forward to seeing what my team thinks."

As Martin described this last strength, his eyes lit up and his voice became higher and more emphatic and energetic. Darren knew that there was something there that they should follow up on. Martin's native genius lay in motivating people, and he was clearly good at it. Martin didn't like rules and being forced to be accountable. He was spending too much time on something he was good at but did not enjoy (meeting numbers using the company's current procedures). Darren was reminded of something he had heard his own daughter say not too long ago: "Just because I can do something, doesn't mean I should." Martin's growth opportunity depended on spending more time in his area of native genius.

"Aha!" Darren said to Martin. "Now we're getting somewhere!"

Action Strategies: Delegate, Delete, Contain

Too often, we spend time on the things we know we are good at just because we know we *can* do them, but they are not necessarily things we enjoy or even the best use of our time. We've identified three options for dealing with those things we are good at, but that drain our energy: delegate, delete, or contain. Here, too, native genius can come to the rescue.

More often than not, once we have defined our native genius, opportunities to *delegate* in those areas arise spontaneously. We see that others are willing and capable of taking on non–native genius tasks, freeing us to move on and focus on work we do prefer. Another strategy is to *delete*—to just stop doing some things altogether. When neither delegation nor deletion is an option, a helpful strategy is to *contain* those tasks: schedule a time to complete the more boring tasks so that you can focus on the good stuff.

Find Your Native Genius

You don't have to wait for a mentoring relationship to find your own native genius. Begin by looking for the intersection of what you do best and what you most like to do. Ask yourself the same sorts of questions Darren asked Martin—your answers may surprise you. Build on your strengths; discover what excites you and what you enjoy. At the same time, be aware of things that drain your energy. If there is something you are good at but don't enjoy, is there an opportunity to teach it to someone else or to delegate that task? Look for opportunities to build on what you love, not what you think you "should" be doing.

Mentors, this is a great opportunity to utilize what you learned about your mentoring partner earlier on. Reflect on what you learn about what motivates your mentee and what your mentee's values are. These will guide you to ask questions that can help them discover their native genius. You can leverage difference by using what you know about your mentee to ask probing questions. How does what they do align with their values? How does it align with their strengths? Do they have an opportunity to act within the zone of appropriateness described in the last chapter? Let's find out what was next for Darren in motivating Martin to find his native genius.

Darren felt more prepared at his next mentoring meeting with Martin. He knew that he needed to get Martin to become self-reflective and to understand where his ability and desire intersected. Cautiously, Darren set the stage for his probing questions, reviewing the purpose of the mentoring relationship and restating the ground rules around confidentiality. He began by framing the purpose of the conversation that he hoped was about to take place.

"I think you may be stuck," Darren told Martin. "I need to better understand what's going on for you, what you are good at and what you enjoy. I'm hoping you'll be open and honest so that we can explore ways to get you unstuck."

Darren wasn't surprised that it took Martin a while to warm up to the conversation. He allowed all the time Martin needed, and paced his questions to encourage him. The extended conversation that ensued turned into the most honest and open conversation the mentoring pair had had thus far.

Learning about native genius is not just an exercise for mentees. Mentors will also find it instructive as they reflect on their own desires and competencies in their mentoring and leadership roles. Through these conversations with Martin, Darren could see possibilities for his own growth and development.

As Darren realized that Martin felt powerless to change, and had lacked the opportunity to claim ownership for his own growth and development, Darren too became aware of his own limitations. He could see that mentoring was going to be a development opportunity for himself as well. He would need to hone his own mentoring skills to foster that same sense of ownership in Martin. He was going to have to learn how to ask different questions, ones that were more probing, supporting, and challenging. He might also need to sit back and consider how to do a better job of putting his own native genius to work.

» YOUR TURN «

1. When you are energized and excited at work, what are you doing?

_____

_____

_____

_____

2. What are you good at?

_____

_____

_____

_____

3. Where does what you do well and what you love intersect? Use your understanding to guide your mentoring conversations and movement forward.

_____

_____

_____

_____

4. What do you do at work that blocks your productivity and excitement?

_____

_____

_____

Expanding Your Perspective

It is exciting to discover your own motivations and capabilities, and to help others discover theirs. Once you do, however, the question arises: Now what? As mentor or mentee, the answer is the same: You must take action. How can you help yourself or someone else take charge of their learning?

Engage in some serious self-reflection. Too often we are locked into our own cultural orientation, a particular way of viewing others' strengths and limitations. Try to determine the nature of the cultural lens you are looking through by asking yourself:

» Why am I seeing things so differently than my mentoring partner?

» What is shaping the way I am seeing things?

» What cultural lens is my mentoring partner looking through that is shaping what they see?

Then go deeper by exploring the answers to the following questions:

» How might someone else see this situation?

» If this situation is the opposite of what I believe is true, how might someone else see it?

» If someone didn't have the same knowledge that I possess, how might they see this situation?

Remember, you are looking to expand your perspective and explore what you might be missing. After you've done this work, seek to bridge differences by communicating to your mentoring partner, "Here's what it's like for me. How is it different for you?"

» YOUR TURN «

1. What more would you like to learn about your mentoring partner?

_____

_____

_____

_____

2. What have you learned lately about yourself?

_____

_____

_____

_____

If you or your mentoring partner has discovered an area of native genius that seems exciting but are having trouble figuring out how to get started, this is another area for deep reflection. Look for cultural differences between mentor, mentee, and workplace culture that may actually be standing in the way of forward movement. Questions for both mentees and mentors might include the following:

» What's stopping you/me from taking charge of this interest? Could there be a cultural issue I'm not seeing?

» Do I/you feel that people higher up in the organization would have issues if I/you moved into this area?

» What is one easy step I/you can take to make this interest a reality at work?

» What is stopping me from supporting my mentee to take action on this?

» What is stopping me from talking to my mentor about my inability to get started on this?

Building Cultural Competency

Martin was working on motivating his team and thinking about delegation—he had a hard time not doing everything himself just to get it done quickly. This was a long-standing issue for him, and it had bubbled up before with his supervisor and never been fully addressed. It was clear to Darren that Martin would not be able to move forward until it was resolved.

The more Darren and Martin learned about each other, the more they began to realize that there were some fundamental differences in the way they viewed their own roles at work, in their motivations, and the way they saw the potential for opportunities. Early on, as they were sizing each other up, they were judging those differences. Darren thought that he'd like to get Martin to think more like him because it would create more opportunities for Martin. Martin was thinking that Darren's view of the world might be better career-wise, but it didn't resonate with him.

Over time, they stopped judging these different approaches. They started to see where there were commonalities in their thinking and to appreciate where there were differences. Now the challenge was how to make the most of those differences so that they could get the mentoring results they were seeking.

The key is in how each person in the mentoring relationship views differences.

The Intercultural Development Continuum

For more guidance on how to address differences, we focus on the first five stages of sociologist Milton Bennett's cultural competency developmental continuum, which spans monocultural mindset to intercultural mindset (Figure 8.1).[68] These are denial, polarization, minimization, acceptance, adaptation. We like this model for several reasons. First, it helps mentoring partners understand how they are viewing the differences between them. Second, it provides guidance on what to do to progress and develop. Third, it can serve as a diagnostic tool when there is lack of understanding. The only way to learn how to bridge difference is to go through each of these steps. Resist the temptation to leapfrog over a stage.

Stage 1. Denial: This first stage is not only about denying differences ("My cultural experience is the only one that is real and valid"). It is also about missing differences ("I don't understand what all the fuss about differences is; there just aren't that many differences among us"). When you are in denial, you don't recognize that even visible differences (such as gender) might influence outlook, worldview, or perspective.

Denial is especially common in a very homogenous environment. When you rarely if ever have the opportunity to interact with someone with visible differences, you are not cued to think about the differences that lie beneath the surface. If you are in denial, your developmental task is to start to recognize that differences exist. (Note: If you are tempted to skip this step in the belief that you are not in denial, that's a clue to explore your perceptions again!)

When one or both mentoring partners are in denial, there will be no true connection or understanding. Even if the mentoring partners identify as the same gender, race, educational background, or area of expertise, there will be nonvisible differences that make a difference. Perhaps these will be in learning styles, generations, values, or motivation, and certainly there will be differences in life experiences and expectations. But when someone is in the denial phase, they don't notice any of these differences and so are connecting in a superficial, often transactional way.

Stage 2. Polarization: In the polarization stage you start to see differences, but you begin by preferentially critiquing and judging them. When you encounter a difference you evaluate that difference to determine whether it is "better" or "worse" than your own cultural preference. For example: "The way I do x is better than the way you do it." "I prefer my orientation to the world to yours." "I don't like the way they look at this." You end up spending time in your head processing the

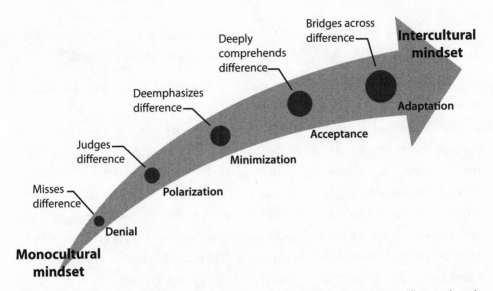

FIGURE 8.1 **Intercultural Development Continuum** SOURCE: Bennett, "Intercultural Communication: A Current Perspective." © 2015–2017 IDI LLC used with permission.

difference in order to judge it from your own cultural vantage point. When you are in polarization, your developmental task is to seek out commonalities.

If one or both mentoring partners is in polarization, they miss the chance for true connection because they are judging the difference rather than seeking to understand it. Curiosity is not present in polarization. Someone in polarization may wonder about another culture, but it is more voyeuristic than from a desire to understand.

Stage 3. **Minimization:** In the minimization stage you're not necessarily judging the differences, but you are deemphasizing the differences from the perspective of your own cultural vantage point. For example: "I see the differences, but they don't really make a difference." "We are all fundamentally the same." In some ways this is what so many of us were taught: minimize differences so that you can connect to the person. Yet if we do not acknowledge the differences between us, we cannot create true connection *because we are not fully seeing or appreciating differing perspectives and experiences.* If you deny an element of someone's culture that is fundamental to their identity, saying "I don't see you as *x*, I just see you as human," the impact on the other person is to feel unseen. The statement "I don't see you as a woman/African American/LGBTQ/etc." is tantamount to "I don't recognize who you are" and "I don't care to understand how that element of your identity shapes who you are," even if that isn't what's meant or intended.

Mentoring pairs in minimization are often blindsided by an issue or challenge that arises from difference. Because they are convinced that differences don't make a difference, when a situation arises where they can't relate to their mentoring partner, they become derailed. When one partner is in minimization, the other partner sometimes is covering or downplaying their own identity so as not to create controversy or conflict. The way we view respect differs by cultural orientation—the way we look at what is kind and nice, the way we look at what our ambitions are, the way we look at authority, the way we look at communication. How we see each other makes a difference. And recognizing that difference is the developmental task essential to getting to the next step: acceptance.

In the first three stages, we've moved along the continuum from not seeing difference (denial) to judging difference (polarization) to minimizing the difference (minimization). These are *ethnocentric* stages, meaning that when you see difference through your own vantage point, you evaluate other cultures according to the standards and customs of your own culture. In an ethnocentric stage you think about difference in terms of your culture. You might ask yourself, "How do people like me see this difference? How is this different than how I see myself?" Often, in an ethnocentric mindset we see difference as something that someone else possesses, rather than something that exists between people. To say that someone else is different makes your orientation normative and someone else's deviant. Cultural competency is about understanding that differences exist between people and that there is no "normal" or "typical" or "right" when it comes to identity and culture.

Stage 4. Acceptance: When you transition into the fourth stage, acceptance, you move from an ethnocentric to an *ethnorelative* viewpoint. You stop evaluating and comparing and begin to approach difference by looking at things from other cultural perspectives. This was the "aha!" for Darren as he began to consider how Martin viewed his circumstance, just as it was for Heather when she began to understand that Aesha's issues with work-life balance were coming from a much more culturally specific place than she had assumed. This fourth stage is a nonevaluative phase. You see how things are viewed from other cultural perspectives. You get that differences make a difference. You understand that there's an imperative for inclusion. You understand that the ability to make meaning depends on seeing that difference. Yet you don't know how to walk the talk. You begin to ask yourself what to do about it. You have great intention and awareness, but you are not yet sure how to implement that intention.

When one mentoring partner is in acceptance, they often feel unable to add value to the mentoring relationship because, although they can see differences and often want to help bridge that difference, they lack the comfort or the skills to do so. We often find that mentors who are in acceptance seek out coaching or the advice of their peers to help them figure out the best way to guide their mentees.

Stage 5. Adaptation: The fifth stage, adaptation, brings us to what Milton Bennett calls "an intercultural mindset." By this stage you are comfortable with many standards and customs, and can adapt your behavior to be culturally appropriate and culturally sensitive. Now you begin to implement the skill of bridging differences, of making that connection, of recognizing the difference, of recognizing where there might be a difference. If you find yourself at this end of the continuum, it does not mean that you know and understand the customs and ways of behaving in every single culture. When people talk about cultural competency, there are many differences you need to be aware of and questions you need to be asking so you can figure it out and relate across culture. If you locate yourself in adaptation, you know what questions to ask. You can operate in different cultures and recognize where people may approach differences.

In adaptation we understand where differences might occur, where our understanding may be incomplete, and what questions to ask to learn about differences. We act as a cultural liaison, helping others to see difference in a nonevaluative way, and as a cultural broker, who can be a go-between who advocates for someone of a different culture for the sake of reducing conflict or producing change.[69] The mentor in adaptation can help their mentee better understand the organization and help the organization better understand the mentee. The mentee in adaptation can help the mentor better understand the mentee's culture or peer group. Their developmental task in adaptation is to continue learning about different cultures and practice the skills of bridging difference to create a win for the mentor partner, mentoring relationship, and organization.

» YOUR TURN «

1. Note where you think you are on the continuum in Figure 8.1. What is your developmental task in order to progress to the next orientation?[70]

---

2. Note where your mentoring partner is on the continuum. If it is the same cultural orientation, what will you do together to develop along the continuum? If your mentoring partner has a different orientation, how will this impact your mentoring relationship?

---

3. What can you and your mentoring partner do to develop your cultural competency?

Working with the Continuum

Let's look again at Figure 8.1. How did Darren try to deepen his understanding about Martin's situation and support him?

Looking at the continuum, Darren would likely place himself in acceptance at the start of his mentoring relationship, moving to adaptation sometime during the year. As an African American man working in corporate America, Darren has been conscious of differences for as far back as he can remember. He didn't want to project his experience with differences onto Martin though, so he made sure to ask questions and acknowledge that Martin's experiences and cultural reference points were different than his.

Darren didn't get too hung up on whether it was his age difference, years of experience, or racial or ethnic identity that were the source of their differences—he just wanted to understand Martin. So, as he listened, he asked a lot of questions. Where it was appropriate, he shared his own stories with Martin, and together they discussed ways that Martin could discover his own strengths and show up authentically. Through these conversations, Darren became more conscious about ABC's policies and practices and how its managers were developing their teams. He started to notice little and big improvements he could implement to improve communication and make the workplace more inclusive.

With Martin's permission, but without mentioning Martin, Darren spoke with Charla, his colleague who oversaw manufacturing and sat on the senior leadership team. Darren had been eager to follow up and find out how manufacturing leadership evaluated performance and what criteria they used. After his conversation with Charla, he felt much better equipped to help Martin understand and navigate ABC's organizational culture and avoid obstacles. Darren and Martin talked about ways Martin could advocate for himself effectively within ABC and still show up as himself.

Martin was grateful for Darren's interest and expertise, and he put his newfound knowledge to use right away. Nonetheless, he soon found himself stuck on a new plateau.

Working on the PIE: Performance, Image, Exposure

During one mentoring meeting, Martin lamented to Darren: "My performance is great. I always meet my metrics. Why aren't I getting anywhere?"

Darren could absolutely relate. He remembered the advice his favorite high school teacher gave him: "Be so good they can't ignore you." Darren knew that performance was only a small piece of the equation, and that the secret to discovering why Martin felt so stuck was in how he was viewed and his exposure to opportunities and even how he viewed himself.

According to Harvey Coleman, author of *Empowering Yourself: The Organizational Game Revealed*, three factors contribute to success in the workplace: performance, image, and exposure (the PIE model). "Performance" is the quality of your work. "Image" is how you are perceived. "Exposure" is about visibility—access to opportunities, to a network, and to people who can advocate for you.[71] In a perfect world, we would be judged 100 percent on performance. However, Coleman's model suggests that performance accounts for only 10 percent of success while 90 percent of an individual's success is due primarily to a combination of image (30 percent) and exposure (60 percent).

It is true that doing a good job is table stakes for success. Without satisfactory performance, we will not get very far. However, the PIE model reminds us that performance will not get you all the way there; in fact, it won't even get you close. We must pay attention to our image, which is influenced by how we show up and by how we are perceived. For mentees, this means looking at how we are presenting ourselves and how that might be perceived. For mentors, this means providing feedback on how mentees are perceived, providing coaching on how to show up authentically and navigate organizational dynamics and customs. For mentors and organizations, this means noticing, managing, and advocating for change in areas where there is conscious or unconscious bias that is unfairly or inequitably working against the mentee.

We must also attend to exposure. Mentoring can make the biggest difference in this area. Mentors can open up their network to their mentee; offer perspective about additional opportunities for work experience or networking; and, with their mentee's permission, advocate for their mentee in situations where the mentee might not otherwise have exposure or access. How did Darren use the PIE model in his mentoring relationship with Martin?

As Darren reflected on the PIE model, he thought of his own privilege. He realized that his long tenure in the organization—more than thirty years—had helped contribute to how his performance was viewed and that had been his ladder to success. Because he had been there such a long time, and because he was in a leadership role, he had a presumed sense of credibility when he spoke. It hadn't been easy, and as an African American man, Darren still did not have the presumed sense of belonging many of his white colleagues had. There were a lot of years early on when Darren was passed over for opportunities, and many meetings to which his white colleagues were invited from which he was excluded. His own mentor had helped him build relationships at ABC. Darren had worked hard to build his network and to nurture it, and over time it had paid off. He had hoped he could now work with Martin to pay it forward a bit.

For his part, Martin realized it wasn't his performance that was holding him back. It was his lack of access to networks. It was his lack of social capital. It was the way he was perceived. He now believed that his colleagues did not understand his cultural differences. They misinterpreted his style of asking questions and his inquisitiveness. Because Martin held the view that if his team didn't rise, he didn't rise, he now realized that he had spent most of his time advocating for his team and not enough time advocating for himself.

Darren was able to help transform Martin's thinking and acting by understanding that there were other critical components that needed to be addressed in order to help Martin succeed. Darren's task was to support Martin by helping him gain exposure and become more aware of his image. Ultimately, because of Darren's position, he was able to influence the organization to become more conscious of how it viewed employees who are traditionally marginalized or underrepresented or who have a nontraditional path.

Here's the lesson of the PIE model: Instead of working together to create a goal that helps an employee do their job better, effective mentoring partners focus their time working on goals that require the mentee to enhance their image or exposure. Is there a particular skill, behavior, or competency they might work on (image)? Can they become more aware of how they are perceived by others (image)? Are there people whom they should meet to expand their network (exposure)? Are there development or job opportunities they might not be aware of (exposure)? Is there a body of work or area of expertise with which they are unfamiliar that might be helpful (exposure)? Framing goals to increase image and exposure is more likely to take into account individual differences and result in more motivation and momentum to the mentoring effort.

Enabling Growth through Support, Vision, and Challenge

How does a mentor help a mentee expand their image and exposure? The mentor's work falls into three facilitation categories. The mentor *supports* the mentee by nurturing and establishing a mentoring relationship that promotes learning and development. The mentor assists the mentee in creating and articulating a *vision,* and moving toward realization of their vision. The mentor *challenges* and motivates the mentee to stretch and gain traction toward achievement of goals. Each of these must build upon their trust and awareness and must leverage the learnings about their mentoring partner to enable meaningful growth.

The mentee's responsibility during this time is to communicate their needs to their mentor. It moves things along if a mentee has thought about what type of support helps them in their learning and what kinds of support they would like to receive from a mentor. What is helpful? What is not? Envisioning a realistic future is often difficult. When it comes to a possible future, most mentees don't know what they don't know. The best advice we give the mentees we work with is to maintain an open mind and communicate openly. When mentees let their mentors know how they like to be challenged, and what's missing from any current mentoring relationship, it can only help their mentor know where, when, and how to offer guidance to them.

Support

For support to be meaningful, it must be the right kind and provided at the right time. This is a formidable task. Mentors need to "get" their mentees, to understand who they really are. Only when mentees bring their authentic selves to mentoring can a mentor bring timely and relevant support for the relationship and learning. This means that mentees need to remain open to learning and be comfortable being themselves (vulnerabilities and all). How did things evolve for Martin as he worked on the guidance Darren provided?

Finally, after six months, things started to improve for Martin. As he continued to work on his Performance Improvement Plan (PIP), he held several conversations with his manager and now felt more optimistic that the expectations his manager had laid out for him were realistic and doable. Once Martin bought in, he was excited to be working more on his own development.

Darren exercised his curiosity. He needed to gather more information before he felt he was in a better position to help Martin realize that Martin was the only one who could change his own circumstances. Finally, Darren and Martin reached a point where they both felt the shift in Martin's outlook and progress. Martin was also getting increasingly curious—the more he learned, the more he wanted to know. Each became more curious about the other. They decided to hasten the process by starting their meetings with a power question that would help them get to know each other even better.

When the mentoring program administrator called Darren to see how things were going, Darren reported, "I am getting to know how he ticks, and I'm learning so much from him about the manufacturing world and what more we can be doing as a company. I am also learning about the thinking of the younger demographic that he represents."

Darren had come to believe that authority and power didn't hold the same value for Martin's generation as it did for his. Like many of his age contemporaries, Martin believed he could and should take on significant responsibility and make a major contribution as quickly as possible. He brought fresh perspectives and could see how they could make a difference. As a mentor, Darren's big "aha" was that he needed to acknowledge what Martin brought to the table, and the only way he could do that was by asking questions to discover who Martin was and the talent he possessed. Darren expressed positive expectations about Martin, not only by showing he was actively listening but also by encouraging him to create a more effective structure for completing his PIP in a more timely fashion.

Things were going along smoothly, and Martin was feeling more energized and optimistic. But then his father passed away unexpectedly, and the shock stopped Martin in his tracks. He had been very close with his father, and he was devastated by the sudden loss. Although he returned to work a week after the funeral, he wasn't the same Martin, not for months. Darren wondered how he could best support Martin during this time. He chose to let Martin lead the way, and they spent a few months of their mentoring time talking about how Martin was coping with his loss.

Darren asked Martin questions about what rituals his family had to mark a loved one's death. He listened as Martin told him about novenas, the prayers that were said during the nine days after his father's death. Martin believed these prayers would protect his father after his death; he was glad that he was able to pray and grieve openly with his family during this time. Martin shared that, in his family's tradition, openly displaying emotions about grief was expected and encouraged.

Sometimes Darren would share his own family's traditions and his experience when his father had died a few years earlier. At each meeting, Darren would ask if Martin was ready to shift to talk about his mentoring goals; each time, Martin would ask to wait just a little bit longer.

Darren wanted to be respectful but also did not want Martin to lose the momentum they had started to build before Martin's father's passing. Darren suggested that they revisit the agreements they had negotiated six months earlier. Instead of meeting every two weeks, they mutually agreed that a short time-out was in order. They agreed to touch base in a month, and they both set a reminder on their calendars.

Vision

When it comes to creating, articulating, and initiating a vision, it is important that mentors have a deep-seated understanding of who their mentee is, where they are in their career trajectory, and what they hold to be meaningful. A mentee will never realize a vision to which they do not feel connected. How did Darren and Martin find their vision?

About six weeks later (nine months after they had started their mentoring relationship), Darren and Martin began to meet again. Martin was feeling better and, to his great relief, was back on track. He had successfully completed his PIP. He was still in manufacturing, but as a result of the work that he and Darren had been engaged in together, Martin discovered he had a real knack and enthusiasm for process improvement, which required motivating others and improving the way things got done.

Darren and Martin worked on Martin's communication and influencing skills so that he would be ready when a role in process improvement opened up. Martin's perspective shifted. He realized that he could add value by developing in place and positioning himself for a new role when it became available. "I have so far to go, but I realize that my success is on me."

Darren wanted Martin to get a sense of what was possible, and he introduced Martin to some colleagues who had different backgrounds, perspectives, and job functions. This shook Martin out of his fixed mindset. His perspective expanded with new possibilities, and he felt less isolated. He began to formulate a vision for himself. He realized that he needed to build broader relationships so he could move out of manufacturing and get a better handle on the skills he needed to develop to realize his vision. He immediately followed up on Darren's introductions and made appointments with each of the people Darren suggested he meet.

Martin began to see Darren not only as his mentor but as a colleague and one of many resources available to him. One day he turned to Darren and said, "I now know what it takes, and I am ready for the challenge."

By expanding Martin's awareness of what might be possible, Darren had helped Martin set a vision for himself that he could get excited about. Notice that Darren did not map out a plan for Martin. Instead, they talked about what Martin might be interested in, and Darren increased Martin's exposure so that Martin could see other options for himself.

For Aesha and Heather, our mentoring pair from earlier in the book, the concept of vision played out in their story in different ways.

Heather saw that Aesha understood the workings of the organization. She collaborated well with others and already possessed a set of technical skills that brought her continued recognition. However, Heather was not sure that Aesha understood the "why" of health care, and she thought it would serve Aesha well to do so. Aesha's work supported those who care for patients, although she was not a direct patient caregiver. Heather realized it might be helpful for Aesha to understand consumer relationship management. Heather didn't feel up-to-speed on all of these aspects, so she suggested that Aesha might want to interview three people who understood these aspects well. That way, she could learn along with Aesha.

Aesha was all for conducting informational interviews with seasoned health-care individuals who might help her understand consumer health-care marketing, the financing of health care that impacts consumer choice, and the upstream/downstream impacts of a single health-care encounter. She realized that she had never really given thought to the people who health care affected. She asked Heather for names of people to contact. Together they made a plan for Aesha to conduct informational interviews and report back on what she learned. Aesha was excited about the opportunity and very pleased with the list of questions she and Heather had generated to guide the interviews.

In both these examples, reaching beyond the known enabled mentees (and their mentors) to enhance their networks and to gain and shift perspectives.

Challenge

Challenge is the third condition that promotes learning during the enabling growth phase. This is when tasks are set. The mentor challenges and stretches the mentee's thinking and sets high standards for reaching the goals. If you are a mentee, your role during this time is to remain open to possibility, to challenge yourself to do things you haven't done before, to take risks and be willing to explore new ways of thinking. Asking questions, even when you think you know the answer, often reveals interesting surprises. As a mentee, it is vitally important to learn to understand what you need and to ask for it. Challenge is not only a time for the mentor to challenge you, but for you to challenge yourself.

Consider discussing the importance of challenge with your mentoring partner. It can be helpful to explicitly give each other permission to explore your differences, which sometimes may result in what feel like difficult conversations. Understand that you will make mistakes and know that when challenge arises, it comes from an intention to understand one another. This will allow you to give each other grace.

Challenge looks different depending on your cultural view of autonomy and authority. Someone with a strong orientation toward authority, for example, may be more inclined to seek and follow specific directions from their mentor. They might seek frequent check-ins to ensure they are accountable and on track. Someone with a strong orientation toward autonomy, however, may find specific direction stifling or intrusive. Accountability will still be useful, but it could be more informal. In either case, mentors and mentees will not know what works until they ask. Helpful questions may be "How shall we check in with one another?" and "What level of detail will be helpful to you?"

Another element of challenge is for the mentor to gently push the mentee out of their comfort zone to try new things. Is there a presentation they can craft? Is there a white paper they can create or a process improvement they can suggest? Is there a new procedure or policy they might recommend? Are there people they should be networking with whom they haven't mustered the courage to approach? Again, mentees will vary in their willingness to stretch. It can be helpful to create space in mentoring meetings for a mentee to "test drive" the challenges they take on. If you both have created a safe space for sharing, your mentoring relationship will also likely be a safe space to experiment. Use your mentoring time to role play, practice a presentation, review and give feedback on a first draft, and so on. Find a zone of comfort that works for both of you. The beauty of the mentoring relationship is that it provides a safe place to take risks and experiment with new possibilities. It becomes easier to accept the mentor's challenge when the mentee can take a test run and practice the new behavior. (Chapter 9 on feedback offers some suggestions on constructive ways to use the "test drive" time.)

Let's look at Aesha and Heather's use of time during their meetings.

Aesha and Heather spent one of their meetings role playing the informational interview session that they had agreed on as a goal for Aesha to learn more about the health-care

industry. Heather had promised to make the most of that time, so rather than just offer a "Good job!" during the role play, she played the role of an unwilling interviewee.

Heather was impressed at how well Aesha was able to handle the situation. She was especially struck by Aesha's ability to ask questions in a way that would help Aesha turn these informational interviews into valuable networking opportunities and connections down the line. Heather thought these learning experiences would also help Aesha in her current role.

» YOUR TURN «
(for Mentors)

1. What are specific examples of things you would do or say to support a mentee?

_____

_____

_____

_____

2. What are specific examples of ways you could help a mentee see, develop, and realize a vision of their future?

_____

_____

_____

_____

3. What are some specific examples of how you might challenge a mentee?

_____

_____

_____

_____

» YOUR TURN «
(for Mentees)

1. What do you need from a mentor to feel supported?

_____

_____

_____

_____

2. What do you want your mentor to say or do to help you see, develop, and realize a vision of your future?

_____

_____

_____

_____

3. When you experience a learning challenge, what helps you tackle it?

_____

_____

_____

_____

In the next chapter we look at some of the problems that mentors and mentees may discover as they try to bridge differences. We explore the importance of providing meaningful and culturally respectful feedback and offer a framework for doing that. Finally, we delve into the nature of mutual accountability.

================ **Chapter Recap** ================

1. One key to understanding your mentoring partner is to determine what lies at the intersection of what they are excited about and what they are good at. This is called native genius.

2. Cultural competency is how we make sense of difference. By recognizing and approaching difference with a sense of curiosity rather than judgment, we can effectively learn from and leverage difference. This is the adaptation phase on the Intercultural Development Continuum (see Figure 8.1). This continuum provides a helpful developmental model for cultural competency.

3. Most career success depends on how we are viewed in the workplace and our exposure to people, opportunities, and resources. Though excellence in job performance is important, it is only a small factor in overall success, and performance goals can be addressed by the mentee's supervisor. Learning in mentoring should focus on improving image and increasing exposure—the two factors that will contribute to most of the mentee's success.

4. Mentees look to mentors to provide support, challenge them, and help them set a vision for success. It is essential to have a discussion with your mentoring partner about what support, vision, and challenge look like for each of you.

NINE

Enabling Growth through Feedback

In the mentoring relationship, constructive feedback is everything. The more a mentee understands the nature of the feedback process, the more they value the feedback that they receive from mentors. The more a mentor understands the value of feedback, the more they can improve their mentoring skills and grow their relationship with their mentee. Keep in mind the following points:

» Feedback facilitates learning, drives mutual accountability, and enables growth.

» Feedback provides mentees with support, offers guidance in creating and articulating a vision, and challenges them to take the next steps in their growth and development.

» Feedback lets mentors know when they have gotten off track, overstepped, missed the point, or provided needed and welcome support.

Although feedback is essentially neutral, and can often be positive, many people tend to hear it meaning "criticism." So when a mentor says, "I'd like to give you some feedback," many mentees hear "I am now going to criticize you." Understandably, they approach the message about to be delivered cautiously instead of welcoming it as an opportunity to improve. Similarly, when a mentee expresses a desire to give their mentor feedback about the mentoring relationship, mentors may hear it as "You are doing a bad job." So rather than welcome the feedback as an opportunity to deepen the relationship, they shut down. It is important to consider how feedback is perceived in your mentoring partner's cultural context. It may be especially important to discuss this with your partner as part of your initial conversations. Because feedback can be so contentious, we recommend having an open discussion about it as part of setting your general parameters and expectations. Discuss what the word means to each of you, and how you can assure each other that in the future any feedback will be meant to be constructive—not critical. Constructive, culturally appropriate feedback is one of mentoring's most precious gifts. Getting and giving honest, candid feedback is a key benefit of mentoring. In fact, the free exchange of frequent feedback is one of the hallmarks of an effective mentoring relationship. Feedback drives mutual accountability. You can use it to check in with your mentoring partner, monitor the relationship, make sure learning is steadily progressing, and honor differences in a way that is consistently meaningful and culturally respectful.

Sometimes course-correcting feedback is simply changing a few words in the way we frame it. A frown, a furrowed brow, and the question, "Would you mind if I give you some feedback you may not like?" implies criticism and will almost surely be taken as such. Talking about "areas of improvement" or "challenges" is one way to avoid the perception of criticism and negativity. Another way is to avoid the feedback word altogether and simply have a conversation that touches honestly on the aspects you want to bring up without casting blame. Giving and receiving feedback is not always easy. Fortunately, this process can be learned (for more on feedback in mentoring, see the resources in the appendix at the back of the book).

In this chapter we take a closer look at how you can use feedback to bridge differences in your mentoring relationship. Giving and getting culturally relevant feedback requires accessing and using your skills and knowledge of each other. Feedback will help you keep your relationship and goal achievement on track and drive better mentoring results. Throughout your relationship you will be seeking it, giving it, and receiving it, so it's important to develop your feedback agility.

What Is Feedback?

Feedback is not a one-way street: mentor and mentee engage in a conversation in which one conveys information back (that is, "feeds back") to the other with an eye toward reinforcing and supporting behavior, improving the mentoring relationship, elevating individual performance, or achieving goals. The partner, in turn, opens to receiving the feedback, and "feeds back" to their partner in the form of clarifying questions or nods of understanding. Feedback should not be passive; rather, it should stimulate further conversation.

Mentees appreciate receiving feedback when they know it is given in good faith, with the intention of improving their performance and supporting their long-term development and career success. Mentees often seek confirmation that they are meeting their mentor's expectations, and feedback can help alleviate a common fear that they may be disappointing their mentor. Mentors can use feedback freely to acknowledge mentees' progress and hard work. Mentors also seek and benefit from confirmation. They depend on mentee feedback to make sure that they are meeting their mentee's needs and expectations. In the absence of feedback, mentors and mentees can find themselves making erroneous assumptions. When that happens, as we've discussed, trust erodes and communication runs the risk of becoming inauthentic.

In our experience, mentors and mentees who commit to building their own competency and confidence in the feedback process report more positive outcomes than those who do not. Mentoring partners who are prepared to engage in a meaningful feedback process have a much easier time overcoming things that are blocking their growth and relationship. The challenge is to stay in conversation and learn from feedback even when it becomes uncomfortable.

Setting the Stage for Feedback

We can remedy the common experience of expecting feedback to be negative and unwelcome by creating an expectation up front for frequent feedback—both positive and negative. Giving and getting feedback may sound straightforward, but it's not, especially when we talk about feedback across cultures. To be effective, feedback must be culturally sensitive and relevant. It is critical to use the knowledge you have gained about your mentoring partner to shape the feedback you give them. In this process reviewing your partner's motivation and expectation can be particularly helpful.

How Is Your Mentoring Partner Motivated?

You've already learned about your mentoring partner's aspirations and why their goals are compelling to them. Mentors, as you think about how to frame your feedback, consider how the behavior that's the subject of your feedback hampers or helps your mentee get closer to their goals and aspirations. If you can tie the feedback to their "why," your feedback will be more resonant and palatable.

What Is Your Mentoring Partner's Expectation about Feedback?

Does your mentoring partner expect positive reinforcement or direct criticism? These expectations vary by culture (consider the cultural continua discussed in Chapter 3). What is your mentoring partner's preference for direct or indirect communication? If feedback is delivered in a way that is not aligned with their cultural orientation, it will be more difficult for the recipient to separate the message from the way it was delivered. As discussed in Chapter 7, the key here is that you find the "zone of appropriateness" that aligns with the cultures of both the person delivering the feedback and the person receiving the feedback.

For years, coauthor Lisa worked in environments where feedback was delivered in a "sandwich" style—something positive is said at the beginning and the end, and something critical in the middle. Since Lisa is more comfortable with direct communication, this never sat well with her. The sandwich approach always felt manufactured and disingenuous. For that reason, when she first delivered feedback to a new colleague, she did not follow the sandwich approach, instead opting to get right to the point by launching into critical feedback. What a mistake! Her colleague bristled and shut down, and it took Lisa some time and effort to repair the working relationship. Later, this colleague told Lisa that she felt in that conversation that all the goodwill she had worked to create had been dismissed and unappreciated.

Effective feedback should identify and reinforce behaviors that contribute positively, while suggesting alternative behaviors for those that get in the way. It is not always easy, however, to be comfortable with the process. Giving any kind of feedback can be fraught with concerns about how the feedback will be taken, fear of damaging the relationship, and the potential for resistance. If one or more mentoring partners tend to be conflict averse, it makes it even less likely that an individual will engage in candid feedback. You need to understand your mentoring partner's comfort with conflict, and their preference for direct or indirect communication. This does *not* mean that you refrain from giving feedback if a mentoring partner is conflict averse, and we caution you not to avoid feedback just because it might feel awkward. Rather, the challenge is to discuss with your mentoring partner how they want to receive feedback and then to provide feedback in a way that is in the zone of appropriateness for their (and your own) cultural preferences.

Apply the "Platinum Rule"

When communicating across differences, we like to replace the Golden Rule (treat others as *you* would like to be treated) with the Platinum Rule: treat others as *they* would like to be treated. Having conversations up front about delivering and receiving feedback gives you valuable information about how to follow the Platinum Rule in the future. In this way you can build trust and avoid feeling defensive or fearful when feedback is offered. If you have skipped over any of the content in Part 2 of the book, "Learn from Differences," you will find seeking and giving feedback to be more difficult. Go back now and have those conversations. It will require work on your part, especially the uncomfortable work of understanding your mentoring partner's perspectives and taking responsibility to bridge differences. There is no shortcut.

» YOUR TURN «

1. How would you describe your level of comfortable in receiving feedback?

_____

_____

_____

_____

2. How do you like to receive feedback? What works for you? What doesn't?

_____

_____

_____

_____

3. How do you prefer to give feedback?

_____

_____

_____

_____

Three Functions of Feedback

Effective feedback serves three functions. It provides your mentoring partner with support, vision, and challenge. Both mentor and mentee can share in these functions.

1. Providing Support

Providing support to your mentoring partner helps in managing the mentoring process. Mentoring partners can provide support in the following ways:

» Listening.

» Sharing authentically.

» Maintaining a climate conducive to learning.

» Expressing positive expectations (for the mentoring relationship and for the learning outcomes).

» Being an advocate for your mentoring partner.

» Creating structure and maintaining accountability.

» Checking in on goals.

» Role playing or test-driving projects.

2. Offering Challenge

Mentors can challenge mentees by giving a gentle push and encouraging them to stretch toward new goals.

» Suggesting things outside of your mentee's comfort zone and providing a safe place for the mentee to take risks.

» Encouraging your mentee to reach out to others to get feedback.

» Setting high standards and acknowledging when they have been met.

» Asking probing questions.

» Engaging in discussion.

» Presenting opposing viewpoints or perspectives.

» Letting your mentee know if they have not stretched enough.

» Asking questions that bring past actions into consciousness and promote insights into change.

» Exposing mentees to new opportunities they are unaware of or lack access to.

Mentees can participate in the challenge by

» Letting your mentor know if you need them to hold you accountable.

» Asking probing questions.

» Engaging in discussion.

» Presenting opposing viewpoints or perspectives.

3. Clarifying Vision

Mentors can clarify or link to their mentoring partner's vision. Clarifying or linking to vision for the mentoring relationship or vision for professional goals is critical because it encourages movement. If you don't know where you are going, you may well encounter missteps, you get stuck, or delay, or put off working on either goals or strengthening the relationship. Here are some ways a mentor can help a mentee crystalize a vision for themselves.

» Fostering ongoing reflection.

» Sharing your story.

» Modeling the way.

» Offering a map and cocreating the steps to the future vision.

» Suggesting what the vision might look like when realized.

» Creating future scenarios.

» Role modeling.

» Holding up a proverbial mirror to encourage mentee self-reflection and heightened self-awareness.

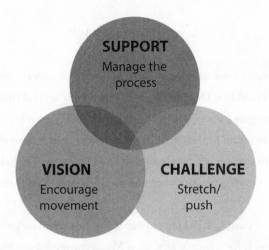

FIGURE 9.1   Three Functions of Mentoring

We repeatedly hear from mentoring partners who have been through our programs that these three functions of the feedback process were critical in contributing to their growth and learning, and made a significant difference in the outcomes of their mentoring relationships. As Figure 9.1 shows, these functions overlap and support each other. It is less important which of these functions your feedback serves than it is that your feedback definitively serves at least one of these functions.

Giving Feedback

Feedback can be given by either the mentor or the mentee (and ideally by both) and should center on the mentoring relationship or the learning goals. The key is that feedback be candid, clear, and (most important) actionable. Best practice is to make time for feedback regularly. Check in on goal progress regarding the mentoring relationship at least once a quarter. This chapter shows you how. (Of course, if the feedback may be of immediate benefit to the recipient, there may be no need to wait for a scheduled meeting session.)

Each of the three mentoring pairs we've been following throughout the book had occasion to seek, receive, give, and address feedback. As we look at their experiences now, it becomes clear that effective feedback is never a one-off event but a regular, consistent expectation in mentoring experiences. Let's begin with Mia and Christopher.

Candid Feedback

Mia expected to receive feedback from Christopher about how she was doing and how top leadership perceived her. Despite asking Christopher several times about how he thought things were going and what he was hearing, all she ever heard was, "You are doing just fine." Mia found it hard to believe that there wasn't something more to work on, and she began to wonder if Christopher was really invested in helping her improve. Soon, Mia started second-guessing what she was hearing from Christopher and stopped asking.

Not too long after that, Christopher appeared somewhat standoffish, almost cold. After thinking about it for a couple of weeks, Mia wondered if she had said or done something that had offended him. In fact, something altogether different was going on. Christopher thought Mia was doing well, and though there were some areas in which he thought she could improve, overall he was quite pleased with her progress and with the mentoring relationship. Lately, however, he had been especially cautious when interacting with his female coworkers. A close colleague of his had recently left the firm after being accused of sexual harassment. It had taken Christopher by surprise, and he wondered if his colleague had been falsely accused. His confidence in how others were perceiving him took a huge hit.

Christopher suddenly became much more reserved, and reluctant to offer feedback. He started second-guessing himself, worried that his trademark warmth might be misinterpreted as flirtatiousness. Guarded, he now hesitated to socialize with his female colleagues or engage in his usual collegial behavior with them. He was particularly cautious with Mia, given that he was her superior in the firm and their mentoring relationship required one-to-one time. Since Christopher had never had a female mentee before, he was unsure how to be authentically warm without seeming inappropriate. His approach was to simply shut down.

Meanwhile, the firm's mentoring coordinator sent out an email to mentors suggesting they do their midyear mentoring check-in at a restaurant over lunch or dinner. Christopher, already walking on eggshells, was uncomfortable about having a meal alone in a restaurant with Mia. Concerned that he would be sending the wrong signals by dining with her alone outside the office and even inviting her to do so, he instead planned on conducting the midyear check-in with Mia in his office.

When several of the mentees in Mia's cohort asked her if she'd had her dinner meeting yet with her mentor, she was puzzled. She hadn't known that was supposed to occur. She wondered why everyone else was having their midyear check-in outside the office. She was getting fed up with Christopher's lack of communication. Mia decided not to wait to discuss this. It was time to bring up her concerns with Christopher. She wanted to know how he felt she was really doing, and whether something had happened to get their mentoring relationship off track. But before Mia could say a word, Christopher made it easy when he asked her how she was doing. She swallowed hard and then proceeded, cautiously.

"Christopher, when we set up ground rules at the beginning," she said, "we agreed that we would give each other feedback. I need some feedback, both on how I'm doing on my goals and on our mentoring relationship. I've heard from several mentees that they have had midyear check-in dinners outside the office. I know you are busy, but I guess I was surprised that this wasn't even raised as an option for us. I've also noticed that lately you seem somewhat distant in our meetings. I am wondering if I've offended you or done something wrong. Or is there a bigger issue in the firm that I need to know about? I'd like to get a handle on what is happening and what I can do to correct the situation. What do you think?"

Christopher felt found out. He wasn't sure how to respond. "I'm sorry about that," he said. "You haven't offended me, and you have done nothing wrong. This is good information for me about how I am coming across to you. In general, I think things are going well, but I do think we should schedule some time to check in and give each other feedback. How about if we dedicate our next meeting to talking about how the mentoring is going and how you are coming along on your goals? Let's come in with ideas on what is working well and what we can improve upon. I'd like to be prepared for that conversation and need some time to do so."

Mia was mollified but still somewhat confused. Christopher thought he'd handled it, but from Mia's reaction he realized maybe he could have handled it more gracefully. Coincidently, he received more unexpected feedback the next day. The week before, Christopher had shared with his friend and former mentee Mike his hesitancy to engage with women in the firm due to his fear that his good intentions might be misconstrued. At the time, Mike had grimaced but said nothing. Mike had thought about the conversation over the past few days, and though he feared compromising his relationship with Christopher, Mike thought it was important for Christopher to understand the problematic implications of his avoidant conduct. He wanted to support Christopher in addressing his behavior sooner rather than later, before it came back to bite him.

Mike suggested that Christopher needed to get over his hesitation in relating to women in the firm and that while his gender sensitivity if understood would be much appreciated, some of the women in the firm were now finding him inauthentic, dismissive, and hard to engage with. "You're a warm guy, Christopher, with a big heart and the best of intentions. Be yourself and be genuine, but you've got to be yourself and be genuine with men and women, and you'll be just fine."

Mike's feedback to Christopher was as tough and uncomfortable for him to give as it was for Christopher to receive. When Mike left Christopher's office, Christopher sighed. He knew Mike was right—he needed to be authentic or he was being unfair to his female colleagues, especially so to Mia. He sent an email to Mia right away: "Let's schedule the feedback meeting for next Thursday lunch at Main Street Grill."

Feedback should be welcomed and given throughout the mentoring relationship. Effective feedback should be aimed at constructively reinforcing and bolstering positive behavior and at changing behaviors that might get in the way of success. Contrary to popular belief, feedback is important to give when things are going well (positive feedback) and when things are not going well (hard feedback).

Positive Feedback

Positive feedback encourages and reinforces good and productive behaviors and results. It can be a great motivator and a catalyst for continued growth. However, people either forget to give it, or deliver it generically as "Great job!" "Way to go!" or "You're doing fine." The problem is, such comments are so vague that the recipient can't replicate the behavior that warranted the positive comment.

Tailor your positive feedback to state *specifically* what was good, and why. What was the impact of the action? The hard work you did in getting to know your mentoring partner will pay off here. Positive feedback should be tailored "to help [your mentoring partner] see, in slow motion, what [their] own personal version of excellence looked like. . . . By helping your [mentoring partner] recognize what excellence looks like for her—by saying, 'That! Yes, that!'—you're offering her the chance to gain an insight, you're highlighting a pattern that is already there within her so that she can recognize it, anchor it, re-create it, and refine it. That is learning."[72]

Coauthor Lois tells the story about a time when she had mulled over a presentation many times, revising it up until the last minute because she didn't want to overwhelm her audience. The program coordinator who had hired her had been very specific about the company's learning needs. After the presentation three participants told Lois that the presentation was spot on and exactly what program participants wanted to hear. They said they appreciated Lois's patience and particularly how she "made them think about new possibilities for themselves and the organization." They went on to say how much they enjoyed her book for mentors and asked her when she was going to write a book for them (they were mentees). Lois asked what questions they would want to see answered in such a book. They spoke and later emailed, and less than a year later, Lois's book *The Mentee's Guide* was published with a table of contents mirroring their questions. The feedback interaction between Lois and the participants served as a win-win. It reinforced her approach and gave her an idea and direction for the content of her next book, and the participants got their questions answered in writing (and a signed copy of the book).

» YOUR TURN «

1. Think about a time you received positive feedback from your mentor or supervisor about something you were doing that was getting in your way. What worked well and what didn't?

   _____

   _____

   _____

   _____

2. Think about a time you gave someone positive feedback about something they were doing that was getting in their way or in your way. What worked and what didn't?

   _____

   _____

   _____

   _____

3. What did you learn from these experiences about how you prefer to receive feedback that you can share with your mentoring partner?

_____

_____

_____

_____

Shielded Feedback

It is easy to fall into the trap of shielding feedback. This happens if we are uncomfortable with giving feedback in general, if we are afraid of hurting another person's feelings, or if we are uncomfortable with conflict and want to avoid provoking it. One way we shield feedback is to withhold or sugarcoat it. In this case, we filter what we say in an attempt to make it "not so bad," rendering the feedback incomplete and ineffective. Sometimes the person on the receiving end is simply puzzled.

Sometimes we hesitate to provide full feedback to protect ourselves from being seen as biased, sexist, racist, or simply insensitive. Or we shield feedback to protect someone else because we fear we might hurt or upset them. Even when we have the best intentions in mind, the desire to protect the other person can make this halfway-home feedback feel inauthentic. It creates misunderstanding that ultimately will erode the trust in your relationship. It stymies growth. If you find yourself wanting to shield your feedback, take the opportunity to explore what's holding you back from being more straightforward.

Hard Feedback

Hard feedback directly addresses the uncomfortable emotional or behavioral issues that impede effective workplace or mentoring performance. Understanding these discomforts makes giving feedback easier. Why is hard feedback so tough? Maybe it stems from our need to be accepted or liked, our fear of reprisal or rejection, or our concern that the relationship will be compromised if we address issues directly.

How to give hard feedback: When you find yourself having to give hard feedback, here are some things to keep in mind.

» **Don't let your own negative triggers get in the way.** Take a deep breath. Don't fly off the handle if your mentor or mentee has done something to anger you. Try to depersonalize your view of the situation. Control your triggers. Remain calm.

» **Begin with the end in mind.** Think about the reason you want to give this feedback. How do you want the mentoring relationship or the other person to behave differently after you have given them feedback? What approach is most likely to elicit that response?

» **State your intention in giving the feedback.** Take time to set the context for giving the feedback. Set up the conversation so it will be supportive. If it comes out of the blue, the feedback can be taken in the wrong way. For example, "I thought we had a pretty good work plan in place. I'm concerned that we haven't made much progress moving things forward. I'm wondering, what's going on for you?"

» **Consider appropriate emotions.** Remember that expressing emotions is viewed differently by different cultures. Some cultures view the display of emotion as weakness; other cultures view expressed emotion as a sign you are invested in the outcome and the relationship, and the withholding of emotion signals that you do not care. How will your mentoring partner view the expression of emotion? How can you manage your own conduct to accommodate for potentially different views about expressing emotion?

» **Speak respectfully at all times.** Be mindful of the Platinum Rule: treat others as *they* wish to be treated. What does respectful communication look like for you and your mentoring partner?

» **Timing is everything.** Make sure your feedback is delivered as soon after an observed behavior as possible. Being attuned to your mentoring partner is important. What is your mentoring partner's mood? How receptive might they be? What current work responsibilities are they managing that might affect their receptivity to your feedback?

» **Think about how you can offer support.** Before delivering the feedback, think about ways you can offer your support. Be sure to ask your mentoring partner what kind of support would be helpful to them so they feel empowered to act on your feedback.

Steps for giving hard feedback: We have found the five steps to giving hard feedback outlined in Table 9.1 to be helpful.

» YOUR TURN «

1. Think about a time you received hard feedback from your mentor, supervisor, or colleague about something you were doing that was getting in your way. How did it go? How did you respond?

_____

_____

_____

_____

2. Think about a time you gave someone hard feedback about something they were doing that was getting in their way or in your way? How did it go? How did you respond?

_____

_____

_____

_____

Seeking Feedback

When trust has been established, mentoring relationships can be an ideal and safe place for feedback. Feedback, even hard feedback, can become especially helpful for mentees to gain perspective on challenges they may face as they go about achieving their goals. Let's look at how Mia dealt with seeking feedback in her mentoring partnership.

Christopher invited Mia to a client meeting where he was preparing a senior executive for a deposition in a high-profile class-action lawsuit. Mia took copious notes, and in her next similar-client meeting, she tried to imitate Christopher's style and approach.

TABLE 9.1 *Steps for giving hard feedback*

Step	What to do	What to say (examples)
1	Talk about what you both gain by having this conversation.	I want to be as successful as I can be in this role. (mentee) We both want to make sure that you achieve your goals. (mentor)
2	Talk about your observations as facts but share your conclusions as your "story."	It has been at least four weeks since we talked. It is hard to get on your schedule. I'm wondering if you still feel our work together is worth your time. (mentee) You acknowledge that planning your team meetings helps you stay organized and ensures you get results. So, when you don't use an agenda or create a plan for your meeting, it leads me to believe that you are really not committed to improving. (mentor)
3	Listen to their "story" to get their perspective.	Is that what's happening, or is it something else? (mentee) What's going on for you? (mentor)
4	Develop new agreements.	What can I count on from you? (mentee) What are you really prepared to do? (mentor)
5	Summarize your agreements in an optimistic way.	So, we've agreed that . . . (mentee) What I take away is that you are going to . . . (mentor)

Source: Authors. © 2019, Center for Mentoring Excellence®

The client was not responsive. In fact, he got angry with her. The client told Mia she was not being "lawyerly" enough.

Mia knew she had bombed, but she couldn't understand why. She asked Christopher to help figure out what she had done wrong. When she explained her approach to him, Christopher told her, "It all sounds good to me. That's what I would have done too. Can you show me how you did it?"

As Mia demonstrated her approach, Christopher recognized that she was mirroring his style. He saw immediately that this approach was all wrong for Mia. "I know you are copying what I did in the deposition prep you sat in on, but it's not working for you. Show me how you would have done it had you never seen me in action."

Mia thought for a minute and then began. She used different words, changed the tone of her questions a bit, and varied her speech. "That's the way to do it!" Christopher exclaimed. "It's more natural for you, Mia." Immediately Mia felt bolstered and more confident in her approach. As Mia was leaving his office, Christopher said: "Go be you next time. Much more effective than trying to be me."

Feedback toward goals can be offered unsolicited by the mentor, or, as in Mia's case, can be solicited from the mentor by the mentee to help increase awareness and improve performance. As the example above shows, when a mentor provides feedback to help a mentee show up authentically, it can serve as a great confidence-booster. This is another situation in which self-awareness and awareness of your mentoring partner is a clear benefit.

Mentors, here are two questions for you to think about: When is your mentoring partner mimicking what they have seen you or others do? How can you help them show up more as themselves?

Getting Better at Giving Feedback

We have observed that mentors and mentees who commit to building their own competency and confidence in the feedback process experience more positive outcomes than those who do not. The first key to giving effective feedback is to speak from your own perspective with the understanding that your perspective is not the other person's reality. Set a context, be descriptive, give examples: the goal is to enable your mentoring partner to clearly see the parallels about how the feedback is relevant to them. For example: "In my experience as an educational administrator (context), I had to earn my reputation by writing successful grants (descriptive example). I know that this is not your exact situation, but maybe there is something to learn here (seeking parallels)."

Table 9.2 provides several feedback tips for better mentoring, for both partners.

TABLE 9.2 *Feedback tips for mentoring partners*

What to do	How to do it	Examples
Mentors: Align your feedback with your mentee's agenda. **Mentees:** Provide feedback about what works for you.	**Both:** Provide real-time feedback. Make it usable and realistic. Offer concrete practical steps and options.	**Mentors:** I have a few ideas that might help . . . **Mentees:** What works for me is . . .
Mentors: Provide feedback about behavior that the mentee can do something about. **Mentees:** Identify incidents where you were seeking help.	**Mentors:** Describe the mentee's behavior rather than succumb to the temptation to evaluate and judge it. **Mentees:** Offer examples of what would have been helpful at that moment in time.	**Mentors:** Tell me about the impact of the behavior **Mentors:** How might someone else see that behavior? **Mentees:** What would have been helpful to me in that situation was . . .
When you talk from your perspective, remember that your reality is not the other's reality.	When you talk about your own experience, set a context and be descriptive so that your mentoring partner can see the parallels.	In my experience, which was . . . , I found that . . . . I know that is not your situation, but maybe there is something to learn here.
Check out your understanding of what is being said.	Listen actively. Clarify and summarize.	If I understand what you are saying . . . Help me understand what you mean by . . .
Demonstrate curiosity.	Seek to understand your mentoring partner's perspective and explore possibilities.	I am curious . . . I wonder if/whether . . . Wait. What?

(continued)

TABLE 9.2 *Feedback tips for mentoring partners (continued)*

What to do	How to do it	Examples
Be aware of your communication style and how that works with that of your mentoring partner.	Share information about communication styles with each other and discuss the implications for the feedback cycle.	I find that I get defensive when . . . I react positively to . . .
Avoid giving feedback or responding when you lack adequate information.	Ask for time to get the information you need. Faking it doesn't work.	To be honest with you, I need to think about that a little more.
Think about feedback as movement forward rather than interruption from the journey.	Continually link progress and learning to the big picture and the journey and learning goals.	When we started out . . . and then . . . and now . . .

Source: Adapted from Zachary, *The Mentor's Guide*, 180, Table 7.1.

Feedback Requires Safety and Trust

Christopher had confidence that Mia was ready for a challenge and decided to advocate on her behalf for an opportunity that he knew would offer her greater experience and exposure. Knowing that Mia was looking for more opportunities to pitch business, Christopher looked out for opportunities for her. He learned about one that was coming up quickly and wasn't sure if Mia could be prepared to pursue the opportunity on such short notice, but he decided to advocate for her to be in on the pitch. The partner in charge agreed, and Christopher called Mia about the opportunity.

"You don't need to take it, Mia. I know you are slammed with work, but I wanted to make sure you had the opportunity."

Mia was thrilled to know that Christopher had advocated for her, but she wasn't able to imagine how she could squeeze it in on such short notice given her existing workload. "I have this big motion to argue next week," she explained to Christopher, "but I can try for it if you think it's a good opportunity." What she really meant, however, was: "I'm so swamped I can't see straight."

Great," said Christopher, "I'll let them know you're in!"

What happened here? Christopher wanted to help Mia get exposure to new opportunities and found an experience he thought would challenge her and raise her profile. In his mind, he gave Mia an out if she was too busy. As someone who values directness, Christopher expected Mia to be direct and turn down the opportunity if she didn't believe she could do it, but Mia didn't want to disappoint her mentor and spoil her chances at future opportunities. This interchange could end up working out well for Mia, or it could be a disaster. The conversation itself was also an indication that Christopher and Mia need to work to build more trust and mutual understanding so they can have more honest communication. Mia and Christopher missed out on a chance for mutual learning by not discussing the significance of the opportunity, whether Christopher thought it was important for her to prioritize it over her current workload, and Mia's concerns about her ability to manage all the work.

Using Feedback to Keep the Relationship on Track

Feedback becomes more complicated, and even more critical, when mentoring partners come from different cultural backgrounds. Mentoring partners must spend additional time understanding their differing perspectives and checking in on the mentoring relationship to make sure it is meeting the expectations and needs of both mentoring partners. As we wrap up this chapter on feedback, let's look at how Aesha and Heather handled these concepts.

Heather started to think through how she could best help her mentee. She wanted to create a structure for them to move forward, so together they created a list of people at Any Healthcare and in the industry whom Aesha could contact to learn more. Aesha and Heather set Aesha's goals to expand her network and awareness of the industry and to conduct informational interviews. They also established a timeline by which Aesha would complete these interviews.

At each of their subsequent meetings, Aesha reported on how the interviews were going and asked Heather questions to help her crystalize her learning. Aesha spent six weeks contacting the names on her list and conducting informational interviews. The interviews went well, and she made significant progress. Heather was impressed with Aesha's efforts and the insights she had shared about the industry, and she told Aesha that explicitly several times.

Aesha was pleased with the plan they had created. The interviews opened her eyes to new perspectives and generated even more questions for her about consumer health-care marketing. As she neared the end of her list, she couldn't wait to share what she had learned with Heather. On the day of their next meeting, however, Aesha arrived at her mentoring meeting feeling particularly tired and frazzled. Although she had been looking forward to sharing her progress with Heather, Aesha was clearly distracted. Heather took notice and asked her about it.

Aesha explained that she was preoccupied with family. Her husband's parents had arrived from India two weeks earlier and this time had decided to stay for four months. Since her in-laws had arrived, Aesha found herself thinking about the ground rules she and Heather had laid out months ago. She wanted to revisit the conversation and ask Heather to reconsider the ground rules about how they structured their meetings so that Aesha could get some advice on balancing work and family.

Heather was surprised by the request. She had thought things were going well—after all, Aesha had been making such great progress on her goals. Heather hated to see Aesha's progress stall out because of a switched focus to family issues. But it was clear that Aesha wanted additional help, and she needed it now, so Heather agreed to switch their focus temporarily. However, she encouraged Aesha to return to their original plan as soon as possible.

Aesha shared that she was feeling frazzled, pulled between work and family. Heather listened for a while. As the meeting ended, Heather switched the focus back to their work plan. She asked Aesha how she felt about their progress so far. Aesha said she was pleased with their progress and appreciated the direction they were headed in. Heather sensed hesitation from Aesha and asked her about it. When Aesha shared her concern about actually implementing their plan in timely fashion given her family obligations, Heather responded, "There are always tough choices you have to make if you want to succeed. You are going to have to set some boundaries." Heather encouraged Aesha to compartmentalize her family issues so she could focus on achieving her goals. Then their meeting time was up.

Aesha left feeling more unsettled than when the meeting began. She had hoped Heather would be empathetic to the pull of family obligations and give practical tips on how Aesha might manage her time outside of work. She concluded that she would have to figure it out on her own. Aesha proceeded to burn the candle at both ends and showed up to their next meeting tired. Her work wasn't suffering, but she still hadn't figured out how to "compartmentalize" while still honoring her in-laws.

Heather took note immediately. She knew what the problem was and could tell that Aesha was distraught. "Aesha," said Heather, "you've been asking me about how to balance work and family life and I'd like to offer some perspective. You've got to stop agonizing over this. Women have been struggling with it forever. I don't have the answer for you. I've been thinking that maybe we should identify a mentor for you to focus just on that."

Aesha, hurt and defensive, didn't understand how Heather could not see work-life balance as part of her overall goals of time management. "I am not complaining. I have an obligation to my family. This is just how Indian culture works. Know that I am trying, as hard as I can, to make it all work."

As a white woman who grew up in the United States with little exposure to cultures other than her own, this was new territory for Heather. She heard something in Aesha's voice that made her pay more attention. "Maybe Aesha was right and I don't understand," Heather thought. She asked Aesha how being an Indian American affects her at work. Aesha shared how much she valued her family's traditions and culture. She loved the way her heritage emphasizes interdependence of family.

"It really grounds me and makes me feel part of something deeply personal and important," Aesha told Heather. She explained that her family was large and multigenerational, and they relied on each other for security, support, and often for social engagements. That warm connection came to life for Aesha each year around the festival of Diwali, held usually in late fall. She explained the festival of lights to Heather and her family's experience of the celebratory event. Aesha and her family would spend most of the day cleaning and decorating the house, then have a big party with lots of food and dancing. Aesha loved this, and wanted to continue many of her family traditions, but she also felt a pull to something more modern and individualistic.

Heather was riveted and asked lots of questions. She, for instance, couldn't understand why Aesha would agree to host her in-laws for so long. Heather's mother used to say: "Always follow the three-day fish rule: after three days fish and guests both start to stink." Heather mentioned this to Aesha.

"Oh no," Aesha said, with a laugh. "Not for my family. We are fiercely loyal and dedicated to each other, particularly to older generations. Asking them to stay for less time or to stay somewhere else would be very disrespectful and viewed as me not honoring my elders and not being a dutiful wife. And I want them to come. But I find myself torn between all the things I want to do for my career and my development, and all the obligations of having extended houseguests."

Heather was now glad Aesha had revisited the scope of their mentoring relationship, and that she was finally learning how to pick up on Aesha's nonverbal cues to go a bit deeper. Heather was surprised at how much she'd learned and how many of her own judgments she'd dispelled in the course of just a few mentoring conversations. Now that she had gotten to know Aesha and her culture better, Heather had a keener insight into the genuine pull that Aesha's family had on her time and Aesha's inability to focus on current work and mentoring tasks.

Heather now understood more about how hard it was for Aesha to balance both family and work obligations. She understood how real and persistent Aesha's feelings of guilt and obligation were. Heather had never faced anything like this. She had always been able to work harder or longer hours whenever she needed. She had always viewed the work itself as meeting her obligation to her family, not tearing her away.

In fact, until meeting Aesha, Heather thought that guilt was just an excuse people used when they weren't fully committed to their career. Heather laughed out loud as she thought about that, feeling guilty herself for any lack of compassion she may have shown to Aesha or any other colleague in the past.

Mutual accountability is an indispensable part of the mentoring process. An accountability conversation is essentially a feedback session designed to check in and make sure the learning and the relationship are on track and moving forward. If you and your mentoring partner haven't previously brainstormed some questions that you want to use for your check-in sessions, use the following suggestions to get started:

» How well are we communicating with one another?

» How can we improve the quality of our mentoring interaction?

» Are there some lurking dangers or "undiscussables" in our mentoring relationship?

» What additional learning opportunities, resources, and venues should we add to enhance the learning experience?

» Are we making time to reflect on our partnership regularly?

» Is the quality of our mentoring interaction satisfactory to each of us?

Chapter Recap

1. Every relationship faces obstacles at one time or another. Acknowledge that in advance and prepare yourself for how you will handle obstacles once they arise.

2. Regular feedback on goal attainment and on the mentoring relationship is essential. If you check in on the partnership and on goal progress at least once a quarter, you will be more likely to create an environment where feedback is welcome.

3. In addition to creating an environment of trust, regular feedback on the mentoring relationship will help ensure that the relationship is a good investment of time and the needs and expectations of mentor and mentee are being met.

4. Always deliver feedback honestly, openly, and in a way that is culturally appropriate for you and for your mentoring partner.

TEN

Coming to Closure

During this fourth phase of the mentoring cycle, you and your mentoring partner take stock of what you learned and make a plan for the future. Coming to closure is more than a quick handshake. Ellen Goodman, a Pulitzer Prize–winning journalist, tackled difficult conversations in founding The Conversation Project to respect people's end-of-life wishes. She offers the following wisdom on the topic of closure: "There's a trick to the 'graceful exit,'" she says. "It begins with the vision to recognize when a job, a life stage, or a relationship is over—and let it go. It means leaving what's over without denying its validity or its past importance to our lives. It involves a sense of future, a belief that every exit line is an entry that we are moving up, rather than out."[73]

Coming to closure thus marks the end of your mentoring relationship as it once was and marks the transition to what it will become. Closure, as Goodman says, is about "moving up, rather than out." Mentoring closure offers a unique opportunity to maximize and leverage learning.

Good Closure

Good closure provides an opportunity to leverage what you've learned; to look back and to move forward, whether you plan to continue your relationship or not. It presents a unique opportunity for reflection, growth, and development for both mentors and mentees. Ideally, closure should always end with an awareness of new opportunities for growth and development. Mentors and mentees who choose to continue their relationship come to closure and recycle through the phases again, hopefully with a deepened relationship. Good closure creates developmental momentum that extends far beyond the life cycle of the mentoring relationship. Mentoring partners often come away with significant and deep learning that is sustainable over time. Think about your mentors, past and present. Chances are your mentors' wisdom still resides within you as a voice in your head.

An early mentor of Lisa's once handed her a copy of a floppy disk bearing the words "My DIG list." She told Lisa that DIG stands for "Damn, I'm good" and suggested Lisa record all her accomplishments throughout her career, whether large or small, so she could learn to self-advocate and get a confidence boost when she needs it. Though Lisa no longer keeps that list, even today when she has a large or small win, she hears her mentor's voice and says to herself: "One to add to my DIG list." Likewise, long ago, Lois's mentor gave her this advice: "Try it. What have you got to lose?" That mentor's wise words still ring in her ears, prompting Lois to take risks and be open to new opportunities.

Good closure offers mentors and mentees an opportunity to take stock and plan for future growth and development. Even if a mentoring relationship has not met your expectations, there is still important learning that can be gleaned from a good closure experience. A good rule of thumb to remember: never close the door to a mentoring relationship without first opening the next door to other development opportunities. Once you've reviewed what you've learned, spend time talking about your future and the next steps in your learning and development journey.

Good closure, regardless of the learning outcomes, should be a positive experience. Both mentor and mentee must come prepared for it, having reflected on the process beforehand. Together, discuss what you learned individually and as mentoring partners. Consider how the mentee might leverage learning and apply what they've learned more strategically, how they may have evolved as a mentor, and even the lessons the mentor has learned from the mentee about enhancing their own mentoring success. Likely you will want to celebrate your achievements, perhaps over a meal, with a toast, or an appreciative letter. Finally, you and your mentoring partner should decide how or if you wish to remain in contact with one another and on what basis. If you do continue to meet, you may decide to continue to meet as before, or going forward to meet on an ad hoc basis, or not at all.

Redefining the relationship helps you and your mentoring partner move on and let go of your relationship as it was and move forward and "up."

In this final chapter we follow the stories of our three mentoring pairs through the five steps in the closure process: (1) planning for closure, (2) reaching a learning conclusion, (3) integrating learning, (4) celebrating, and (5) redefining the relationship and moving on.

Planning for Closure

It may seem unnecessary, but it's important to prepare for closure just as you prepared for mentoring before your first meeting with your mentoring partner. If closure is to be a mutually satisfying learning experience, you must plan and prepare for it with your mentoring partner. Spend time creating a shared sense of progress as you bring your relationship to a close. Whether you are a mentor or mentee, preparing in advance for the final mentoring meeting will help you both maximize and leverage your learning. Allowing adequate time to prepare will permit you both to further accelerate your learning, achieve better outcomes, and have a more satisfying and productive closure experience. When you plan and prepare well for closure, the learning payoff is huge. Let's look at how Mia and Christopher planned for closure.

Mia and Christopher had been meeting for nearly a year when they scheduled a meeting to bring their mentoring year to closure. They expected that they would continue to meet as mentor and mentee and decided that they wanted to take time to reflect on what they had learned during their mentoring year. They each came to their closure conversation with a list of what they had learned. Independently, each had set aside time to reflect on the partnership, the learning process, and their learning outcomes.

Mia had hoped Christopher would help her shape her career and position her for consideration as a partner when the time was right. She wasn't disappointed, and was grateful for his time and wisdom. Certainly, Christopher had challenged her thinking and offered her a variety of opportunities to meet and work with the other partners in the firm. She felt she was well on her way to meeting her career goals, with lots of new ideas.

Mia reflected on the goals they had set at the beginning. The first was identifying and building ten potential clients or referral sources. She felt good about what she had achieved. Although she didn't reach her target goal of ten sources, the eight relationships she did solidly build were an accomplishment she could take pride in. Her second goal—to increase her self-awareness about how she was perceived by her peers and potential clients—had been more challenging. Mia realized that she wasn't finished working on self-awareness. She knew that if she wanted to be successful, this would require a lifetime of attention. She took out her laptop and began her list of what she had learned.

- » To slow down when I am speaking.
- » How and when to speak with authority.
- » To be specific in asking for what I need.
- » To trust myself more.
- » To check out my assumptions.
- » To become more open to new experiences.
- » To listen more attentively.
- » Sometimes I am just too much all business.

Mia reviewed her list one last time before she closed her laptop and put it in her tote bag along with a book she had purchased that she thought Christopher would like.

Christopher couldn't believe how fast the year had flown by. He recalled his initial reluctance in accepting the assignment of mentoring a young woman and realized now how much he would have missed out on if he hadn't followed his friend Mike's advice to fully engage in mentoring. He had learned about his own biases and prejudices, become more aware of generational differences, and now saw how what he had learned could be leveraged to help expand and grow the firm.

When Christopher started his list of what he had learned, he expected to have time to add to it before he met with Mia. Time ran out, but that didn't stop him from making a mental list of all that he had learned.

- » Increased awareness of generational perspectives.
- » Influence of culture on my behavior.
- » How assumptions frame my actions.
- » Increased self-awareness from peer feedback.
- » Importance of asking the right questions at the right time.
- » The value of being authentic.
- » Not to let fear stand in the way of mentoring or supervising women at the firm.

» YOUR TURN «

1. How will my mentoring partner and I ensure that our relationship reaches a positive learning conclusion?

_____

_____

_____

_____

2. What would I like to see happen when our mentoring relationship ends?

_____

_____

_____

_____

3. How will my mentoring partner and I structure our final meeting?

_____

_____

_____

_____

Reaching a Learning Conclusion

Reaching a learning conclusion is an indispensable part of coming to closure. It can help mentoring partners articulate what made the mentoring experience worthwhile. It validates both the mentor and the mentee that their mentoring time was well spent and a good investment in the mentee's future. A learning conclusion is a focused conversation in which mentoring partners reflect on their learning, their relationship, and the mentoring process. The goal is to flesh out specifics about what you've learned during your experience together. This conversation is central to bringing about satisfying closure. If you skip over it, you may miss an opportunity to learn more about yourself or about mentoring. This should be a no-fault conversation about the specific learning that you and your mentoring partner have derived from your mentoring experience.

Let's see how Darren and Martin's final meeting went.

At the end of the yearlong mentoring program, Darren and Martin prepared for their final meeting by reflecting on their experience during the past year. Martin shared that he felt his communication skills had improved. He had developed the habit of using constructive language with his team and had been receiving positive feedback from the very people who had been on his case before. Off the top of his head, he could think of three examples of times he had applied his new communication skills.

It was huge for Martin to realize that just because he could do something, didn't mean that he should. His growth opportunity depended on spending more time on things that he was good at and liked doing. He realized that if he wanted to move out of manufacturing, he needed to build broader relationships. If he developed more relationships, he could get a better handle on skills he needed to develop to realize his vision and pursue the opportunities that might be available.

Martin had been struck by something Darren explained to him about the framework of "low context" communication. That concept had been entirely new to Martin, but he understood it immediately. It made him think about how he liked and needed lots of information to understand things; it made him realize that his coworkers might actually be overwhelmed by his barrage of questions. Martin's translation of his new awareness into different behaviors made a huge difference in how others related to him in the workplace.

Darren recalled Martin being stuck in a viewpoint about his future that he couldn't seem to shake, and he recalled the meeting when they both felt the shift in Martin's outlook and progress. Martin had been getting increasingly curious, and that was a good thing—the more he learned, the more he wanted to know.

Darren had come to realize that expectations about career advancement were different for Martin than they had been for himself. He suspected this reflected a generational difference. Like many of his age contemporaries, Martin believed he could and should take on significant responsibility and make major contributions as quickly as possible to show others that he deserved increased responsibility. For Darren, this felt a bit foreign, because he had always believed that increased responsibility came with time, title, and age. Martin had brought fresh perspectives to the relationship that Darren could now appreciate, and he saw now they could make a difference.

As a mentor, Darren's big "aha" was that he needed to acknowledge what Martin brought to the table, and the only way he could do that was by asking questions to discover who Martin was and the talent he possessed.

» YOUR TURN «

1. What was the most valuable thing you learned from your relationship?

\
\
\
\

2. In what ways have you grown and developed since this mentoring relationship began?

\
\
\
\

3. What worked particularly well for you and your mentoring partner in this relationship?

\
\
\
\

4. What might we each do differently the next time we engage in a mentoring relationship?

\
\
\
\

Integrating Learning

Integrating learning is about setting an intention to take what you have learned and leverage it. It is another value-added aspect of the closure process. In addition to all the benefits and purposes noted at the outset of the chapter, the intention of closure is to provide an opportunity to process and integrate what you've learned, enhance those learnings, build on them, leverage them, and ultimately maximize them. How did Darren integrate his learning from the mentoring partnership going forward?

Darren gained new perspectives and knowledge as a result of mentoring Martin. As a baby boomer, Darren hadn't understood at first why Martin had gotten so upset by having to follow work rules like putting in "face time"—spending a certain amount of time at work even if he could finish the job faster working remotely instead of having to clock in and the like. Rule-following, after all, had been one of the key factors in Darren's success. Once Darren understood that these rules seemed senseless to Martin, and therefore felt confining and disrespectful, Darren started to approach things differently. He wondered if his organization ought to review and update its work rules if it wanted to avoid losing younger talent like Martin. Darren wanted to reach out to the leaders in manufacturing, to work internally to build a more inclusive company and see what was holding back some of their employees.

Clearly, Darren saw mentoring as part of his leadership responsibility and now was even more committed to strengthening and diversifying the leadership bench in his organization. Once he did his homework, he became a cultural broker and looked for ways to bring his newly acquired knowledge and exposure back to the executive team. Because of his position, Darren ultimately was able to integrate his learning by influencing the organization to become more conscious of how it viewed employees who were traditionally marginalized or underrepresented or who had a nontraditional career path. And how did Martin integrate his learning going forward, after the year of mentoring?

Martin's thinking had shifted as well. Even though he had met many of his mentoring goals, he was keenly aware that he still had a long way to go. True, he had built allies, in addition to Darren, who would serve as resources for him. Yet the realization that "it is all on me now" landed heavily and shifted his perspective. It was a big step for him to realize that his success and goal achievement was ultimately his responsibility. He found himself setting ground rules and checking in with his team regularly, which seemed to make everyone more efficient and productive. Darren had taught him how utilizing the talents of each team member created synergy and reinforced how important it was to get to know each member of the team.

Here's how Mia and Christopher integrated their learning.

Mia continued to build her book of business. She realized that if she wanted people to bring their business to her, she needed to become a trusted adviser. She was making more frequent presentations in the business community and, as a result, was being asked to sit on higher-profile boards. Targeting her ideal clients had helped her lead authentically and confidently.

Christopher, too, had learned about the value of being authentic and building trust. Rather than running away from difference, he now sought to understand it. He became more understanding of others and more trusting of himself. He found himself asking more questions and searching out opportunities to work with a more diverse group of associates.

» YOUR TURN «

1. How will I apply what I've learned?

_____

_____

_____

_____

2. What will I do as a result of what I've learned?

_____

_____

_____

_____

3. How will I sustain my learning and keep the momentum moving forward?

_____

_____

_____

_____

Celebrating

An important part of closure is expressing appreciation to your mentoring partner. If you feel gratitude, it is a lovely gift to give. Even if you have mixed feelings about the outcome, it is important to express your appreciation for the time and effort your partner put into the process. Just as in all other phases of the mentoring relationship, it is wise to be mindful of cultural differences in expressing thanks. In most Western cultures, saying thank you is welcomed, and even expected, as a way to express gratitude and appreciation. Not offering thanks is perceived as rude or insensitive. However, in other cultures, including some Chinese, Filipino, or Indian cultures, doing nice things for friends and family is expected; an expression of thanks can be perceived as creating a formality between giver and recipient, or suggesting that the "giver" did something out of duty rather than desire. Be sure you know your partner's cultural preferences before having the closure conversation, and mark closure in a way that is culturally appropriate for both partners.

Gratitude needn't be a grand gesture. Consider a small memento or a written note of thanks. Some sincere words can go a long way. One mentor told us that their last meeting was lunch outside the office, during which his mentee took out a letter he had written and read it to him. The mentee described all the ways he had grown during his mentoring year and what he had learned. Profoundly moved, the mentor had no idea he had made that big a difference to his mentee. Mentors often tell us, "I don't need thanks." To that, we say, the thank you may be a need of the mentee, and we encourage mentors to allow mentees to express thanks to you if they wish to do so. Mentors, too, may want to express appreciation to mentees. We encourage you to think in advance about what that will look like. Aesha showed her gratitude to Heather and celebrated the mentoring partnership in a way that was meaningful to her.

Aesha had a hard time figuring out how to express her appreciation to Heather. By the time their mentoring year was up, she was grateful to Heather for so many things. The more she reflected on their relationship, the more she realized how much she had benefitted from Heather's wisdom and counsel. There was so much she wanted to say, and she didn't know if she could say it all in a face-to-face meeting without getting emotional. She decided to write a letter.

Dear Heather,

I want to express how much I appreciate your help and support his year. I feel really privileged to have had you as my mentor.

It was so kind of you to share your amazing career story with me. I was blown away by how much you have accomplished. I learned a lot from your story. As you know, it gave me pause for thought and raised many questions for me. I admire your courage. You started out at a time when there were no mentors for you, with a son to support on your own, and fashioned your own path. Your courage has been a great life lesson for me.

I remember how reluctant I was to jump in and ask questions in the beginning. The mere thought of asking you questions made me nervous. I guess I felt intimidated, and I know I wasn't yet comfortable taking the reins in our conversation given your position at Any Healthcare and how much you are respected. Now I am not intimidated, and I am so much more comfortable. I am much more aware now of when I'm being reluctant to ask for what I need. And that, coupled with your encouragement, has encouraged me to speak up.

What stands out for me, and perhaps what I appreciate most, was your sincere interest in understanding me and my cultural context. When you started asking questions about my family and my background, it meant the world to me. It was then that I felt you really got me and understood my extended family issues and the pressure I was under because of them.

You've helped me see that I can accommodate my family responsibilities and fulfill my work responsibilities without guilt—that I need to take better charge of my time at home and at work, and that I do have a choice in how I spend that time. I so appreciate you sharing your own family's ideas about guests. It made me so much more aware of the many ways there are to live, and I feel very grateful to have had this insight.

I can see now that there are no easy answers, and that I am going to have to work at putting away the guilt and—whether I'm with family or at work—just, as you said, "Get at it!"

I've picked out this Mysore scarf for you as a way of saying thank you. Its aqua, teal, and indigo design reminded me of our mentoring year. The colors start off boldly and separately and then gradually blend together toward the middle, and expand in a swirl. It's kind of a metaphor for our time together. I hope you like it. It is only a small token. Someday I hope to give back to others the way you have given to me. I will be forever grateful to you.

Most sincerely,

Aesha

Aesha's letter and gift had both surprised and gratified Heather. It also set her thinking about how much more culturally mindful she had become since mentoring Aesha. Heather was keenly aware that she had had cultural blinders on before this experience and a lot of unconscious bias about prioritizing work over family that she had come to grips with.

Heather had developed a consciousness about her own cultural lens. She hadn't known how much her lens had limited her viewpoints, yet she now saw that she had been judging others because of that bias. Recognizing this led Heather to become more compassionate. She was surprised to realize that this softening had made her better able to relate to members of her own team and her colleagues, and she felt her other work relationships getting deeper too. The experience had stoked her curiosity and her desire to learn more about other cultures. She was now thinking about taking a trip to India next year, and Aesha had extended her parents' hospitality to host Heather.

Celebrating mentoring should be meaningful and special. To be meaningful, it must be comfortable and unforced. It also needs to be time-sensitive and context-sensitive: Is the timing right? Is there adequate time? Is the setting comfortable? Celebrating should create value and for that to occur, it must be genuine.

» YOUR TURN «

1. How can we meaningfully celebrate our mentoring relationship? How can we make it special?

_____

_____

_____

_____

2. What did I appreciate about my mentoring partner?

_____

_____

_____

_____

3. How will I express my appreciation?

_____

_____

_____

_____

Redefining the Relationship and Moving On

By the time you come to closure, you certainly aren't in the same place as when your relationship began. The obvious next question is, what's next for you two? One or both of you may want to continue the relationship, even if it is in a different capacity. Be proactive and talk about these changes before they take place.

If you are continuing your relationship with your mentoring partner, having a closure conversation at the end of the mentoring year will allow you to reflect on your mentoring experience and cycle back through on a deeper level. It provides an opportunity to review the agreements and parameters you set at the start of your relationship. That is, did the ground rules work for you? What more would you want to add? Were there boundaries that were crossed during the year? How did your confidentiality agreements work for you? What progress did you and your mentoring partner make on your goals? Will there be new goals, or will you continue to work on the same goals? How did the feedback process work for you? What might you want to do differently?

Your relationship with your mentoring partner will be different once the mentoring relationship ends. You may decide to continue and reengage in the present relationship. You may decide to meet on an ad hoc basis, or more informally, or not at all. Once you have redefined your relationship, it is time to let go of the relationship as it was and embrace it as it will be.

Christopher and Mia Plan to Continue Their Mentoring Relationship

During their closure conversation, Christopher and Mia declared their first year as mentoring partners a resounding success. Mia was by now doing high-level work and getting recognition at the firm for her business development efforts. But her mentoring goals had only been partially fulfilled. Mia and Christopher had each become more self-aware during their year, and their conversations had become more authentic. As Mia found her own voice, Christopher realized that he didn't have to have the answers but could help her just by asking the right questions. Although Mia was making progress, they agreed that they had more work to do to achieve Mia's goals. They laid out a plan to go forward.

First, they would revisit the ground rules they had set about meeting frequency, time, and place. Next, they would talk about confidentiality and boundaries. They had learned about each other's triggers, and Mia had gotten much better at slowing down the pace of her speech. Christopher had become more open and frank with Mia. They decided that they needed to incorporate two new ground rules, one about checking out assumptions before acting on them and another about being authentic. They would revisit their mentoring agreement and particularly drill down on the goals they had set. Finally, they would get to work, again.

As they were finishing up their conversation, Mia reached into her tote and brought out the wrapped package she had brought with her and handed it to Christopher. It was *Notorious RGB: The Life and Times of Ruth Bader Ginsburg*, a book about the US

Supreme Court Justice, that Mia had read and loved.[74] She hoped that Christopher would appreciate it as well and looked forward to discussing the book with him down the line.

Aesha and Heather Look for a New Mentor for Aesha

Aesha and Heather discussed whether to continue their mentoring relationship. Though they had learned a lot from each other, they each came to the same conclusion: they would end their mentoring relationship at this time. The suggestion not to continue came from Heather, who thought it would be a good idea because she had a very busy year ahead and some lofty professional development goals of her own. She knew she wouldn't be able to dedicate the time to Aesha that Aesha deserved.

Heather's suggestion took Aesha a bit by surprise. Aesha's natural inclination was to continue because she believed strongly in maintaining long-term relationships and knew she still needed a mentor to make more progress on her chosen career path. Once she thought about Heather's suggestion though, she realized that she could continue her relationship with Heather in a different form. She came around to the conviction that she could find another mentor. Perhaps, since she only had time for one mentoring relationship right now, she would find a mentor outside of Any Healthcare so she could gain broader industry perspective. When Aesha asked to stay in touch, Heather agreed immediately, and they decided to schedule lunch together once a quarter.

Aesha had given some thought about who she thought might make good mentors for her and ran her list by Heather. Heather was concerned that the individuals on the list might not have the capacity or experience to take Aesha to the next level, and she told Aesha so. Heather suggested that they take a step back to develop some criteria for Aesha's choice based on what she wanted to learn and what characteristics she was looking for in a mentor. They developed a list, and both Aesha and Heather added more names. They then evaluated who might be the best fit for Aesha at this time. Two potential names were identified, and Heather offered to make introductions for Aesha.

Heather's experience had been so positive and different from her other mentoring experiences that she too decided to find her own mentor. As she looked to achieve her own goals the coming year, she realized that she hadn't had a mentor in a long time and having the support of a mentor could be invaluable in improving her approach and effectiveness. She wanted to learn how other mentors functioned and what more she could learn from being a mentee again. She, too, decided to look for a mentor outside the organization and turned to an international leadership organization for a mentoring match.

Darren Becomes an Occasional Adviser for Martin

Even though their formal mentoring relationship was ending, Martin realized he was still going to need some advice from Darren. He had just learned that he was being considered for a product analyst role outside of manufacturing and was thrilled about it. At the same time, he was feeling guilty that he might be leaving his coworkers behind. Now that he had a better relationship with his manufacturing leaders, he wanted to handle his exit in a way that would keep the relationships with his team and his leaders intact. This was a new problem to discuss with Darren. Martin was so grateful that Darren had left the door open for some as-needed advice. He scheduled a time for the two of them to get coffee, and Martin decided he would be the one to buy the cappuccinos this time.

Mentoring is a critical part of personal growth and development and affords a lifetime of opportunity to grow and develop. Redefining mentoring relationships helps both mentor and mentee to bring closure to their experiences and, most important, to learn from them. It also allows partners to circle back and potentially reconnect comfortably years after a mentoring relationship has ended.

» YOUR TURN «

1. How will your mentoring relationship be different after it has concluded?

_____

_____

_____

_____

2. If you plan to reconnect with your mentoring partner, how will that happen?

_____

_____

_____

_____

3. What is the next step you need to take to further your development and growth?

_____

_____

_____

_____

Chapter Recap

1. Whether you are a mentor or mentee, preparing in advance for the final mentoring meeting will help maximize and leverage your learning.

2. To be meaningful and relevant, the closure process you engage in with your mentoring partner must be culturally appropriate.

3. Look toward the future in coming to closure. Once you've reviewed what you've learned, spend time talking about the future and the next step in the mentee's learning and development journey. Consider the implications for the mentor's growth and development as well.

4. Evaluate how your current agreement worked for you before you choose to continue in the same relationship. Avoid the temptation of jumping right back in without reflecting on your prior experience together. You may find that you want to revise your agreements.

A CLOSURE CONVERSATION
WITH OUR READERS

Dear Reader,

Every ending should be the start of a new beginning. Now that you've finished reading *Bridging Differences for Better Mentoring*, we invite you to look back and reflect on your practice and move forward to leverage your learning with new insights. We've learned a lot about our own assumptions while writing this book, and we hope you've taken away some new cultural understandings that will help you in working with the many different people you will encounter every day of your working life.

In moving through the cycle of mentoring in the context of cultural competency, we have focused on exploring many of the differences that exist between mentoring partners. We have done this not to point out how different we all are (though we are!), but with an eye toward promoting greater understanding, strengthening mentoring relationships, and facilitating deeper learning. We believe by bridging differences—that leaning forward into the differences between you, learning from them, and leveraging them—you will find the transformative magic in your mentoring relationship.

We invite you to share your insights with those in your own work environments. Creating mentoring relationships that bridge difference will lead to workplaces that bridge difference. We firmly believe that's how change happens.

Thank you, and good luck on your journey. Keep building bridges!

Lisa and Lois

APPENDIX

Assessments for Personality and Learning Styles

CliftonStrengths. Differentiates your unique strengths and provides guidance on how to best develop these. www.gallupstrengthscenter.com/product/en-us/10108/top-5-cliftonstrengths-access?category=assessments.

DISC Personality Test. Examines behavioral differences that focus on work productivity, teamwork, and communication. Needs to be administered by a qualified administrator. www.thediscpersonalitytest.com/.

How to Fascinate, by Sally Hogshead. Looks at how you are perceived. Focuses on how to develop your unique differentiator. www.howtofascinate.com/get-my-profile/assessment.

Kolb Learning Style Inventory. Examines how you take in and process information. We use version 3. Available from multiple sellers from amazon.com. See https://www.amazon.com/Kolb-Learning-Style-Inventory-V3-1/dp/0000202924/ref=pd_lpo_sbs_14_t_2?_encoding=UTF8&psc=1&refRID=T6BZC0DF2RGWD6T95ZPK.

Resources on Feedback

Chandler, M. Tamra, and Laura Dowling Grealish. *Feedback (and Other Dirty Words): Why We Fear It, How to Fix It*. Oakland, CA: Berrett-Koehler, 2019.

Zachary, Lois J. *Creating a Mentoring Culture*. San Francisco: Jossey-Bass, 2005 (see pages 129–36).

Zachary, Lois J. *The Mentor's Guide*. San Francisco: Jossey-Bass, 2012 (see chapter 7).

Zachary, Lois J., and Lory A. Fischler. *The Mentee's Guide*. San Francisco: Jossey-Bass, 2009 (see pages 92–97).

NOTES

1. Lois J. Zachary, *The Mentor's Guide* (San Francisco: Jossey-Bass, 2012); Lois J. Zachary, *The Mentee's Guide* (San Francisco: Jossey-Bass, 2009); Lois J. Zachary, *Creating a Mentoring Culture* (San Francisco: Jossey-Bass, 2005); and Lois J. Zachary and Lory A. Fischler, *Starting Strong* (San Francisco: Jossey-Bass, 2014).

2. Anjali Shaikh, Kristi Lamar, Kavitha Prabhakar, and Jessica Sierra, "WSJ/ Deloitte Insights Cracking the Code: How CIOs Are Redefining Mentorship to Advance Diversity and Inclusion," *Wall Street Journal*, April 28, 2019, 13.

3. Zachary, *Creating a Mentoring Culture*; Zachary, *The Mentee's Guide*; and Zachary, *The Mentor's Guide*.

4. Zachary, *The Mentee's Guide*.

5. It should be noted that there are other four-phase mentoring models. One of the earliest of these was defined by Dr. Kathy Kram in her 1988 book *Mentoring at Work*. Her model, based on observed psychological and organizational factors, is linked to phases that include longer time frames.

6. Please note that Christopher and Mia's story, like all the mentoring stories in this book, are fictional. They are based on a composite of the hundreds of mentoring partners we have worked with over decades.

7. The Center for Mentoring Excellence coaches and tracks progress of mentors and mentees through its Touch-Base Coaching Interview protocol. For more information, see www.centerformentoring.com/benefits-of-touch-base-interview-tbi -coaching-sessions-our-new-mentoring-offering-now-available.

8. Joseph J. Distefano and Martha L. Maznevski, "Creating Value with Diverse Teams in Global Management," *Organizational Dynamics* 29, no. 1 (2000): 45–63.

9. Andrés Tapia, *The Inclusion Paradox* (Lincolnshire, IL: Hewitt, 2009), 12.

10. Milton J. Bennett, "Intercultural Communication: A Current Perspective," in *Basic Concepts of Intercultural Communication: Selected Readings,* edited by Milton J. Bennett, 1–20 (Yarmouth, ME: Intercultural Press, 1998), 7.

11. Claudio Fernández-Aráoz, Andrew Roscoe, and Kentaro Aramaki, "From Curious to Competent," *Harvard Business Review* (September 2018), https://hbr.org/2018/09/curiosity#from-curious-to-competent.

12. According to journalist Arianna Huffington, this quote is widely attributed to Wayne W. Dyer, but even he has said he's not sure where it comes from. He uses it in his videos and presentations.

13. Elizabeth Bernstein, "Why We Stereotype Strangers," *Wall Street Journal*, October 29, 2018, www.wsj.com/articles/why-we-stereotype-strangers-1540824439?mod=searchresults&page=1&pos=1; Ellen Berscheid and Elaine H. Walster, "Rewards Others Provide: Similarity," in *Interpersonal Attraction* (Reading, MA: Addison-Wesley, 1969), 69–91; Ellen Berscheid and Harry T. Reis, "Attraction and Close Relationships," in *Handbook of Social Psychology*, fourth edition, vol. 2, edited by D. T. Gilbert, S. T. Fiske, and G. Lindzey (New York: McGraw Hill, 1998), 193–231; and Donn Byrne, *The Attraction Paradigm* (New York: Academic Press, 1971).

14. Michelle Obama, *Becoming* (New York: Crown Publishing Group, 2018).

15. Zachary, *The Mentee's Guide*, 18.

16. Bruce G. Barnett, R. J. Mathews, and G. R. O'Mahoney, *Reflective Practice: The Cornerstone for School Improvement* (Victoria, Australia: Hawker Brownlow Education, 2004).

17. Fons Trompenaars and Charles Hampden-Turner, *Riding the Waves of Culture: Understanding Diversity in Global Business,* 3rd edition (New York: McGraw-Hill Education, 2012), 8.

18. Trompenaars and Hampden-Turner, *Riding the Waves of Culture*, 108.

19. Trompenaars and Hampden-Turner, *Riding the Waves of Culture*, 12.

20. See, e.g., Karen K. Myers and Kamyab Sadaghiani, "Millennials in the Workplace: A Communication Perspective on Millennials' Organizational Relationships and Performance," *Journal of Business Psychology* 25 (2010): 225–38.

21. Susan Zemke, Claire Raines, and Bob Filipczak, *Generations at Work* (New York: Amacom, 2013), 82.

22. Zemke, Raines, and Filipczak, *Generations at Work*, 116.

23. Zemke, Raines, and Filipczak, *Generations at Work*, 141.

24. J. M. Twenge and S. M. Campbell, "Generational Differences in Psychological Traits and Their Impact on the Workplace," *Journal of Managerial Psychology* 23 (2008): 862–77, http://doi:10.1108/02683940810904367; and J. M. Twenge and S. M. Campbell, "Cultural Individualism Is Linked to Later Onset of Adult-Role Responsibilities across Time and Regions," *Journal of Cross-Cultural Psychology* 49 (2018): 673–83, http://doi:10.1177/0022022118764838.

25. R. Fry and K. Parker, "Early Benchmarks Show 'Post-Millennials' on Track to Be Most Diverse, Best-Educated Generation Yet," Pew Research Center, November 15,

2018, www.pewsocialtrends.org/2018/11/15/early-benchmarks-show-post-millennials-on-track-to-be-most-diverse-best-educated-generation-yet/.

26. David Kolb, *The Kolb Learning Style Inventory* (version 3.1) (Boston: Hay Group, 2005). We are aware that newer versions of Kolb's Learning Style Inventory are available. However, we find version 3.1 most useful for training mentors and mentees because of its simplicity.

27. There is research evidence that learning styles, as used to determine mode of instruction or study in the field of education, do not exist. See, e.g., Kelly MacDonald, Laura Germine, Alida Anderson, Joanna Christodoulou, and Lauren M. McGrath, "Dispelling the Myth: Training in Education or Neuroscience Decreases but Does Not Eliminate Beliefs in Neuromyths," *Frontiers in Psychology* 8 (August 2017), article 1314. We use learning style as a tool to help participants discover how they best take in and process information and how that might differ from their mentoring partner. We find Kolb's concepts useful in an effort to maximize the efficiency of the mentoring relationship.

28. A quick word about the difference between "stereotype" and "archetype." In this book we provide some information about cultural patterns associated with different geographies or identities. We do this to deliver helpful information that comes from an aggregation of experience and data that helps identify differences. These are archetypes. They are categories that are made to identify themes and patterns that come from broad data and experience. In contrast, biases arise from stereotypes—generalizations that are made from insufficient data or lack of experience and applied to a broader group. In short, archetypes are used to identify themes and patterns based on broad data.

29. See chapter 3 of Mahzarin R. Banaji and Anthony G. Greenwald, *Blindspot: Hidden Biases of Good People* (New York: Bantam Books, 2016).

30. Find out more about the Implicit Association Test at https://implicit.harvard.edu/implicit/aboutus.html. The IAT is available at https://implicit.harvard.edu/implicit/takeatest.html and takes approximately ten minutes to complete.

31. Mary-Frances Winters, *We Can't Talk about That at Work!* (Oakland, CA: Berrett-Koehler Publishers, 2017), 36.

32. Winters, *We Can't Talk about That at Work*, 36.

33. Peggy McIntosh, "White Privilege: Unpacking the Invisible Knapsack," *Peace and Freedom Magazine* (July–August 1989): 10–12.

34. McIntosh, "White Privilege," 10–12.

35. Milton, "Intercultural Communication: A Current Perspective," 7.

36. The figure was developed at the Center for Mentoring Excellence and is described in Lois J. Zachary and Lory A. Fischler, *Starting Strong: A Mentoring Fable* (San Francisco: Jossey-Bass, 2014), 65–169, 166.

37. Stephen D. Brookfield, *Becoming a Critically Reflective Teacher* (San Francisco: Jossey-Bass), 2.

38. Fernandez-Araoz, Roscoe, and Aramaki, "From Curious to Competent," 61.

39. Fernandez-Araoz, Roscoe, and Aramaki, "From Curious to Competent," 61.

40. Adi Ignatius, "Cultivate Curiosity." This article is the online introduction to a series of articles on curiosity in the September–October 2018 edition of the *Harvard Business Review,* see https://hbr.org/2018/09/cultivate-curiosity.

41. Francesca Gino, "The Business Case for Curiosity," *Harvard Business Review* (September–October 2018): 48–57.

42. Gino, "Business Case for Curiosity," 50.

43. For a list of power questions to connect with your mentoring partner, visit www.centerformentoring.com/QuestionsForConnecting.

44. James E. Ryan, *Wait, What? And Life's Other Essential Questions* (New York: Harper One, 2017).

45. Ryan poses two additional questions in *Wait, What?* that we have not addressed here. The fifth question asks "What truly matters?" His sixth question, which he calls the bonus question, quotes Raymond Carver's poem "Late Fragments." Ryan asks: "And did you get what you wanted from this life, even so?" (see Ryan, *Wait, What?* 133).

46. Ryan, *Wait, What?*, 26.

47. Ryan, *Wait, What?*, 36.

48. Ryan, *Wait, What?*, 82.

49. Ryan, *Wait, What?*, 84.

50. "Seek First to Understand" is Habit #5 in Stephen Covey's *The 7 Habits of Highly Effective People* (New York: Simon & Schuster, 1989).

51. David Livermore, *Leading with Cultural Intelligence: The Real Secret to Success,* second edition (New York: Amacom, 2015).

52. Shalini Misra, Lulu Cheng, Jamie Genevie, and Miao Yuan, "The iPhone Effect: The Quality of In-Person Social Interactions in the Presence of Mobile Devices," *Environment and Behavior* 48, no. 2 (2016): 275–98, https://doi.org/10.1177/0013916514539755.

53. Albert Mehrabian, *Silent Messages,* first edition (Belmont, CA: Wadsworth, 1971).

54. These definitions come from Daniel Nettle, *Personality: A User Guide* (Open University, 2013) (accessed on September 21, 2019).

55. For more on MBTI, see www.myersbriggs.org/my-mbti-personality-type/mbti-basics/home.htm?bhcp=1. For more information on judging/perceiving, see www.myersbriggs.org/my-mbti-personality-type/mbti-basics/judging-or-perceiving.htm\.

56. Andy Molinsky, *Global Dexterity* (Boston: Harvard Business Review Press, 2013), 14–15.

57. Molinsky, *Global Dexterity*, 15.

58. Molinsky, *Global Dexterity*, 15.

59. For a more in-depth discussion of ground rules, see chapter 5 of Zachary, *The Mentor's Guide*.

60. Trompenaars and Hampden-Turner, *Riding the Waves of Culture*, 101.

61. Trompenaars and Hampden-Turner, *Riding the Waves of Culture*, 108.

62. Marshall Goldsmith and Mark Reiter, *Triggers* (New York: Crown Business, 2015), 44.

63. Gino, "Business Case for Curiosity," 55.

64. Much has been written about SMART goals, and the acronym itself has several similar definitions. For example, in some models "action-oriented" is interpreted as "achievable," "realistic" stands for "relevant," and "timely" becomes "time-bound." The concept is likely attributable to Peter Drucker's *Management by Objectives*, but even that is debatable, since many others have adapted the acronym.

65. Berwick is quoted in Chip Heath and Dan Heath, *Switch: How to Change When Change Is Hard* (New York: Broadway Books, 2010), 22.

66. Liz Wiseman, *Multipliers: How the Best Leaders Make Everyone Smarter* (San Francisco: HarperCollins, 2010), 47.

67. Authors' personal communication with Kristen Wheeler, founder and creator, Native Genius www.NativeGenius.com, May 3, 2019. To learn more about the Native Genius Method, see www.nativegenius.com.

68. Bennett, "Intercultural Communication: A Current Perspective."

69. Mary Ann Jezewski, "Culture Brokering in Migrant Farmworker Health Care," *Western Journal of Nursing Research* 12, no. 4 (1990): 497–513.

70. You can use our summary of the Intercultural Development Continuum to determine where you are on the continuum. Or you can take an assessment called the Intercultural Development Inventory (IDI). To take an assessment, contact Lisa Fain as a qualified administrator at lfain@centerformentoring.com or find a qualified administrator through the IDI website, www.idiinventory.com.

71. Harvey Coleman, *Empowering Yourself: The Organizational Game Revealed*, second edition (Bloomington, IN: Author House, 2010).

72. Marcus Buckingham and Ashley Goodall, "The Feedback Fallacy," *Harvard Business Review* (March–April 2019): 92–101.

73. Ellen Goodman's last "Endings and Beginnings" syndicated column is found at www.seattletimes.com/opinion/ellen-goodmans-last-column-looking-backward-looking-forward/, originally published January 1, 2010, in the *Seattle Times*.

74. Irin Carmon and Shana Knizhni, *Notorious RGB: The Life and Times of Ruth Bader Ginsburg* (New York: HarperCollins, 2015).

REFERENCES

Banaji, Mahzarin R., and Anthony G. Greenwald. *Blindspot: Hidden Biases of Good People*. New York: Bantam Books, 2016.

Barnett, Bruce G., R. J. Mathews, and G. R. O'Mahoney. *Reflective Practice: The Cornerstone for School Improvement*. Victoria, Australia: Hawker Brownlow Education, 2004.

Bennett, Milton J. "Intercultural Communication: A Current Perspective." In *Basic Concepts of Intercultural Communication: Selected Readings*. Edited by Milton Bennett, 1–20. Yarmouth, ME: Intercultural Press, 1998.

Bernstein, Elizabeth. "Why We Stereotype Strangers." *Wall Street Journal*, October 29, 2018. www.wsj.com/articles/why-we-stereotype-strangers-1540824439?mod =searchresults&page=1&pos=1.

Berscheid, Ellen, and Harry T. Reis. "Attraction and Close Relationships." In *Handbook of Social Psychology*, 4th edition, volume 2. Edited by D. T. Gilbert, S. T. Fiske, and G. Lindzey, 193–281. New York: McGraw Hill, 1998.

Berscheid, Ellen, and Elaine H. Walster. "Rewards Others Provide: Similarity." In *Interpersonal Attraction*, 69–91. Reading, MA: Addison-Wesley, 1969.

Brookfield, Stephen D. *Becoming a Critically Reflective Teacher*. San Francisco: Jossey-Bass, 1995.

Buckingham, Marcus, and Ashley Goodall. "The Feedback Fallacy." *Harvard Business Review* (March–April 2019): 92–101.

Byrne, Donn. *The Attraction Paradigm*. New York: Academic Press, 1971.

Carmon, Irin, and Shana Knizhni. *Notorious RGB: The Life and Times of Ruth Bader Ginsburg*. New York: HarperCollins, 2015.

Coleman, Harvey. *Empowering Yourself: The Organizational Game Revealed*. Bloomington, IN: Author House, 2010.

Covey, Stephen. *The 7 Habits of Highly Effective People*. New York: Simon & Schuster, 1989.

Distefano, Joseph J., and Martha L. Maznevski. "Creating Value with Diverse Teams in Global Management." *Organizational Dynamics* 29, no. 1 (2000): 45–63.

Dweck, Carol S. *Mindset: The New Psychology of Success*. New York: Ballantine Books, 2006.

Dyer, Wayne D. *The Power of Intention: Learning to Co-create Your Work Your Way*. Carlsbad, CA: Hay House, 2006.

Fernandez-Araoz C., A. Roscoe, and K. Aramaki. "From Curious to Competent." *Harvard Business Review* (September–October 2018): 61. https://hbr.org/2018/09/curiosity#from-curious-to-competent.

Gino, Francesca. "The Business Case for Curiosity." *Harvard Business Review* (September–October 2018): 48–57. https://hbr.org/2018/09/cultivate-curiosity.

Goldsmith, Marshall, and M. Reiter. *Triggers: Creating Behavior That Lasts: Becoming the Person You Want to Be*. New York: Crown Business, 2015.

Goodreads. "John Dewey." www.goodreads.com/quotes/664197-we-do-not-learn-from -experience-we-learn-from-reflecting.

Heath, Chip, and Dan Heath. *Switch: How to Change When Change Is Hard*. New York: Broadway Books, 2010.

Ignatius, Adi. "Cultivate Curiosity." *Harvard Business Review* (September–October 2018). https://hbr.org/2018/09/cultivate-curiosity.

Jang, Sujin. "The Most Creative Teams Have a Specific Type of Cultural Diversity." *Harvard Business Review* (July 2018). https://hbr.org/2018/07/the-most-creative -teams-have-a-specific-type-of-cultural-diversity.

Jezewski, Mary Ann. "Culture Brokering in Migrant Farmworker Health Care." *Western Journal of Nursing Research* 12, no. 4 (1990): 497–513.

Kolb, David. *The Kolb Learning Style Inventory* (version 3.1). Boston: Hay Group, 2005.

Kram, Kathy. *Mentoring at Work: Developmental Relationships in Organizational Life*. Glenview, IL: Scott, Foresman, 1988.

Livermore, David. *Leading with Cultural Intelligence: The Real Secret to Success*, 2nd edition. New York: Amacom, 2015.

Louissant, Obed. "Diversity without Inclusion Is a Missed Opportunity." *TD Magazine* 71, no. 2 (2018): 33–37.

McIntosh, Peggy. "White Privilege: Unpacking the Invisible Knapsack." *Peace and Freedom Magazine* (July–August 1989): 10–12.

Mehrabian, Albert. *Silent Messages*. Belmont, CA: Wadsworth, 1971.

Millar, Margaret. *The Weak-Eyed Bat*. Garden City, NY: Doran & Co., 1942.

Misra, Shalini, Lulu Cheng, Jamie Genevie, and Miao Yuan. "The iPhone Effect: The Quality of In-Person Social Interactions in the Presence of Mobile Devices." *Environment and Behavior* 48, no. 2 (2016). https://doi.org/10.1177/0013916514539755.

Molinsky, Andy. *Global Dexterity: How to Adapt Your Behavior across Cultures without Losing Yourself in the Process*. Boston: Harvard Business Review Press, 2013.

Morrison, Terri, Wayne A. Conaway, and George A. Borden. *Kiss, Bow or Shake Hands*. Holbrook, MA: Bob Adams, 1994.

Myers, Karen K., and Sadaghiani Kamyab. "Millennials in the Workplace: A Communication Perspective on Millennials' Organizational Relationships and Performance." *Journal of Business Psychology* 25 (2010): 225–38.

Nettle, Daniel. *Personality: A User Guide*. The Open University, 2006. www.open.edu/openlearn/body-mind/psychology/personality-user-guide (accessed on September 21, 2019).

Obama, Michelle. *Becoming*. New York: Crown, 2018.

Palmer, P. J. *On the Brink of Everything: Grace, Gravity and Getting Old*. Oakland, CA: Berrett-Koehler Publishers, 2018.

Ryan, James E. *Wait, What? And Life's Other Essential Questions*. New York: Harper One, 2017.

Shaikh, Anjali, Kristi Lamar, Kavitha Prabhakar, and Jessica Sierra. "Cracking the Code: How CIOs Are Redefining Mentorship to Advance Diversity and Inclusion." *WSJ/Deloitte Insights* (2019): 13.

Tapia, Andrés. *The Inclusion Paradox: The Obama Era and the Transformation of Global Diversity*. Lincolnshire, IL: Hewitt, 2009.

Thomas, Roosevelt, Jr. *World Class Diversity Management: A Strategic Approach*. Oakland, CA: Berrett-Koehler Publishers, 2010.

Trompenaars, Fons, and Charles Hampden-Turner. *Riding the Waves of Culture: Understanding Diversity in Global Business*. New York: McGraw-Hill Education, 2012.

Winters, Mary-Frances. *We Can't Talk about That at Work!* Oakland, CA: Berrett-Koehler Publishers, 2017.

Wiseman, Liz. *Multipliers: How the Best Leaders Make Everyone Smarter*. New York: Harper Business, 2010.

Wiseman, Liz, Lois N. Allen, and Elise Forster. *The Multiplier Effect: Tapping into the Genius Inside Our Schools*. Thousand Oaks, CA: Corwin, 2014.

Zachary, Lois J. *Creating a Mentoring Culture*. San Francisco: Jossey-Bass, 2005. *The Mentor's Guide*. San Francisco: Jossey-Bass, 2012.

Zachary, Lois J., with Lory A. Fischler. *The Mentee's Guide*. San Francisco: Jossey-Bass, 2009. *Starting Strong*. San Francisco: Jossey-Bass, 2014.

Zemke, Susan, Claire Raines, and Bob Filipczak. *Generations at Work*. New York: Amacom, 2013.

ACKNOWLEDGMENTS

We acknowledge each other with love, admiration, and deep gratitude. It is rare indeed that a mother and daughter get to collaborate professionally. What a privilege it has been for us to coauthor this book. We encouraged each other to bring our own special magic to *Bridging Differences for Better Mentoring* and were able to weave our individual subject matter expertise and varied experiences together to create a book that reflects and elevates our individual strengths and our passions.

We acknowledge Naomi Sigal, our sage and savvy development editor, whose candor and skill made this book better at every step. We acknowledge our publisher, Berrett-Koehler, and its editorial staff. We especially thank Neal Maillet, editorial director, for his encouragement, support, and immediate trust in the process. To Jeevan Sivasubramaniam, managing editor, who was ever ready with prompt answers to our questions and guidance in our process. To Valerie Caldwell, associate director of design and production, for your patience and hard work in art direction for our cover. Many thanks to Eileen Eisen-Cohen for her technical assistance.

We acknowledge our amazing communities of family, friends, colleagues, and clients for their encouragement along the way. Please know how much we are indebted to you all.

Lest we forget, we acknowledge Mia and Christopher, Aesha and Heather, and Darren and Martin—amalgams of the very real mentoring partners with whom we work. We hope their stories will inspire you to draw lessons that relate to your own mentoring relationships.

INDEX

Page numbers followed by n *indicate note, those followed by* t *indicate table, and those followed by* f *indicate figure.*

ABOUT THE AUTHORS

 **LISA Z. FAIN** brings a rich and varied background to her work as CEO of the Center for Mentoring Excellence. She is highly regarded for her special combination of leadership development knowledge, diversity and inclusion expertise, humor, and a no-nonsense practical approach.

Lisa holds an undergraduate degree in social policy and a law degree from Northwestern University. She practiced law for thirteen years, first as a labor and employment law litigator at a major multinational law firm and then as in-house labor counsel at Outerwall, Inc., the former parent company to automated retail giants Coinstar and Redbox. While at Outerwall, she created and then transitioned to senior director of diversity and inclusion.

Under Lisa's leadership, the Center for Mentoring Excellence serves a diverse and broad array of clients, including global corporations, associations and NGOs, world-class law firms, professional sports franchises, and not-for-profit community organizations. Lisa consults with CME clients, helping them to create more inclusive work environments and to develop, establish, and deliver best-in-class mentoring programs. A frequent keynote speaker in the United States and Europe, Lisa sits on the boards of the International Mentoring Association and Military Mentors.

Lisa lives in Mercer Island, Washington, with her husband and two teenage daughters.

LOIS J. ZACHARY is an internationally recognized expert on mentoring and the founder of Leadership Development Services, LLC, and its Center for Mentoring Excellence. She earned her doctorate in adult and continuing education from Columbia University and master's degrees from Columbia University and Southern Illinois University.

She is the author of multiple books on mentoring. Her first book, *The Mentor's Guide* (2000), has become a primary resource for organizations interested in promoting mentoring for leadership and learning and for mentors seeking to deepen their mentoring practice. With *Creating a Mentoring Culture* (2005), *The Mentee's Guide* (2009), the second edition of *The Mentor's Guide* (2012), *Starting Strong* (2014), five *Mentoring Excellence Pocket Toolkits*, and hundreds of articles and blogs, Lois has created a comprehensive set of resources for promoting her lifetime passion: mentoring excellence for individuals and organizations.

Lois's innovative mentoring approaches and expertise helping leaders and organizations design, implement, and evaluate learner-centered mentoring programs have been used globally by a wide array of clients, including Fortune 100 companies, NGOs, government organizations, educational institutions, and numerous profit and nonprofit entities.

For more information about mentoring coaching, consultation and programs, please contact the authors at:

Lisa Z. Fain, CEO, Center for Mentoring Excellence
LFAIN@CENTERFORMENTORING.COM
WWW.LINKEDIN.COM/IN/LISAZFAIN/
TWITTER: @LZFAIN @C4MENTORING
INSTAGRAM: @LZFAIN

Lois J. Zachary
LZACHARY@CENTERFORMENTORING.COM

Berrett–Koehler
Publishers

Berrett-Koehler is an independent publisher dedicated to an ambitious mission: *Connecting people and ideas to create a world that works for all.*

Our publications span many formats, including print, digital, audio, and video. We also offer online resources, training, and gatherings. And we will continue expanding our products and services to advance our mission.

We believe that the solutions to the world's problems will come from all of us, working at all levels: in our society, in our organizations, and in our own lives. Our publications and resources offer pathways to creating a more just, equitable, and sustainable society. They help people make their organizations more humane, democratic, diverse, and effective (and we don't think there's any contradiction there). And they guide people in creating positive change in their own lives and aligning their personal practices with their aspirations for a better world.

And we strive to practice what we preach through what we call "The BK Way." At the core of this approach is *stewardship,* a deep sense of responsibility to administer the company for the benefit of all of our stakeholder groups, including authors, customers, employees, investors, service providers, sales partners, and the communities and environment around us. Everything we do is built around stewardship and our other core values of *quality, partnership, inclusion,* and *sustainability.*

This is why Berrett-Koehler is the first book publishing company to be both a B Corporation (a rigorous certification) and a benefit corporation (a for-profit legal status), which together require us to adhere to the highest standards for corporate, social, and environmental performance. And it is why we have instituted many pioneering practices (which you can learn about at www. bkconnection.com), including the Berrett-Koehler Constitution, the Bill of Rights and Responsibilities for BK Authors, and our unique Author Days.

We are grateful to our readers, authors, and other friends who are supporting our mission. We ask you to share with us examples of how BK publications and resources are making a difference in your lives, organizations, and communities at www.bkconnection.com/impact.

Dear reader,

Thank you for picking up this book and welcome to the worldwide BK community! You're joining a special group of people who have come together to create positive change in their lives, organizations, and communities.

What's BK all about?

Our mission is to connect people and ideas to create a world that works for all.

Why? Our communities, organizations, and lives get bogged down by old paradigms of self-interest, exclusion, hierarchy, and privilege. But we believe that can change. That's why we seek the leading experts on these challenges—and share their actionable ideas with you.

A welcome gift

To help you get started, we'd like to offer you a **free copy** of one of our bestselling ebooks:

www.bkconnection.com/welcome

When you claim your **free ebook**, you'll also be subscribed to our blog.

Our freshest insights

Access the best new tools and ideas for leaders at all levels on our blog at ideas.bkconnection.com.

Sincerely,
Your friends at Berrett-Koehler

Certified

Corporation